TRAINING
YOUR
HORSE OR PONY

TRAINING
YOUR
HORSE OR PONY

by

Diana Goldstone BHSII T

Distributor:
NIMROD BOOK SERVICES
PO Box No. 1
Liss, Hampshire, GU33 7PR
England

ISBN 0 947647-43-0

SBN 1	2	3	LOC.	COPY
94 7647	43	0	I	1

EDITION DATE	1985
CLASS NO.	798-23

INVOICE PAR 16·10·85 £9·50

Publisher:
NIMROD BOOK SERVICES
(Fanciers Supplies Ltd.)
P.O. Box 1
Liss, Hants, GU33 7PR

CONTENTS

MONOCHROME ILLUSTRATIONS

DIAGRAMS

ACKNOWLEDGEMENTS

Cover Photograph — My thanks to Sarah Bruton for allowing me to use this lovely photograph of her riding *Astley Alvere*, better known to his friends as "Alfie". Also the photographer Clive Hiles in Figure 12-3.

For their help with photographs may I thank: Bill Bruton, Hayley Merrett and Kiln Saddlery, R. Putt, and Roger Sparrow, and for allowing themselves to be photographed: Pippa Brown, Bill Bruton, Chris Bussey, Penny Campbell and Alan Watts. Other photographs by the author.

May I extend my gratitude also to Nicola Bull and Pat Gaskin as well as the Colne Valley Riding Stables for the use of their indoor school and Carol Vallis for the use of her arena.

I should like to thank Alan Watts for his Foreword and for the help and encouragement he gave me.

April 1985   *D. Goldstone*

FOREWORD

by

Alan Watts

When Diana Goldstone asked me to write a foreword to her book my feelings were rather mixed. I felt flattered that she wanted me to do it but, at the same time rather nervous like I feel when I ride a dressage competition. After all, I said to myself, she knows so much more about the subtle interrelations of rider and horse than I; maybe my foreword will not do her book much good.

On reflection, however, I realised that a foreword from someone on the *other* side of the fence who has benefitted so much from her methods of teaching, might not be out of place. After all, I did encourage her to write this book in the beginning, and have done what I can to help it along. As well as that, she opened up a whole new world of exploration and understanding for me and one which was so solidly based that I have been able to build up my rapport with, and feel, on a horse on my own from the lessons she has drilled into me in the past.

Diana's task with me and my 14.2 Welsh Cob was a formidable one but she guided and drove me through my problems into that bright land beyond the ability to walk, trot and canter where the subtleties of balance can be added to the ability to produce impulsion. First she got the horse going forward and then she got me to go with it beating each problem as we came to it with her own characteristic methods. In effect Diana said to me "If you have a problem and the classic methods of beating it do not work then try something else — as many different things as are needed to get your horse to respond to you."

It is this breadth of approach that makes the book she has written so different and so useful to the serious person who wants to make progress with their riding. You cannot learn to ride a horse without sweat, toil and tears — and sometimes blood — but so many people working on their own or with a modicum of help have to endure all that without actually making the progress they feel they should have done. That is very frustrating and it is also something which though fundamentally important, is not put right by many books on how to ride a horse.

This book I am sure fills and brightens that grey area between the early days of riding lessons when you are learning how to stay on and the much more precise world of preliminary and novice dressage. One of the recurrent faults I found with books I read to try to improve my riding was the sudden and immense leap there appeared to be between the first part of the book where things were explained in a way that could be understood by a complete newcomer, and the latter parts in which movements such as half-pass and passage were described. These latter things require so much more balance and feel if they are to be done correctly that no way could anyone have made the giant leap from one class of riding to the other. It is to fill that immensely important gap that Diana Goldstone has written this book and I am sure that those who use it conscientiously and read the spirit of it as well as the letter will be able to bridge the often seemingly unbridgeable divide that separates the "young" rider from the "more experienced" rider.

It is generally agreed, throughout the relevant horse world that, the standard of dressage in this country leaves much to be desired and some of this must stem from early training when getting the horse's head at the right "on-the-bit" angle by any means seems more important than painstakingly working through to the same result by application of the aids and learning to create impulsion and so the ability to go forward into a restraining hand.

I am sure that Diana has herein bridged the gap and will set many on the right road from the start so that they become riders of horses rather than devotees of gadgets which produce short-cuts to the "correct" outline, but which build the rider's hopes of progress on insecure foundations so that in the end the whole edifice comes tumbling down.

I know that in writing this Diana had very much in mind the inevitable gaps in the training programme of people who are not professional riders. Her book can be picked up and put down at whatever stage of training you have reached. She has catered for the competitive and the non-competitive alike in her approach and I am certain that no one who reads and applies the substance of this book will not be able to say that they have not been helped towards the goal we all strive for — complete harmony between horse and rider.

Alan Watts

INTRODUCTION

RIDING AS A SPORT

The scope of this book is to cover the basic training of the horse and rider. It is about the flatwork and early jumping which forms a sound basis from which riders can progress to more advanced riding in any sphere of equestrianism. The emphasis is on promoting the forward riding of the horse in all situations. Riders are given suggestions and ideas which will help them towards a greater understanding of how they can make more of their horses. The photographs used in this book are of riders going through the same problems as the readers are likely to be experiencing.

Riding is one of the fastest growing sports in Britain today. It is no longer an elitist sport but within the range of most people's pockets in some form or other. You may ride only at weekends at a local riding school, or go on a trekking holiday once a year; maybe you are lucky enough to own your own horse and can ride most days.

For the more competitive minded there are many kinds of events organised by local clubs to suit riders of all standards. For information about Pony Clubs and Riding Clubs, write to the British Horse Society, Stoneleigh, Warwickshire. Incidentally, many local clubs arrange instructional sessions for their members as well as social events, evening lectures, etc.

Only a handful of riders can ever hope to reach the top of their chosen sport whether it be show jumping, dressage, combined training, racing or whatever. There are many hundreds of others however, who achieve great personal satisfaction at a more moderate level.

This book sets out to help those who wish to improve their riding and schooling ability. I shall explain as directly and simply as possible the effect the rider's position and aids have (or do not have) on his horse. In order that the rider may succeed in giving his horse a good basic education, he must have some knowledge of what to expect from his horse and how to cope when he does not seem to respond to the aids. With the aid of photographs and diagrams, I can explain how the rider may work effectively towards a harmonious partnership with his horse.

THE IMPLICATIONS OF OWNING A HORSE OR PONY

Of the many thousands of horse owners in this country, many are novice or relatively inexperienced. Strangely, unlike owning a dog, a horse does not at present need to be licensed, although this must surely at some point be considered. Licensing would take some years to implement, for to track down all animals kept in unlikely and unsuitable places would be a mammoth task, and indeed for whom? There is much cruelty in the horse world, often caused by sheer ignorance. I have seen a great deal of this in my travels. Caring owners seemingly oblivious to the basic needs of an animal who can do virtually nothing for itself and is entirely at the mercy of our tender care.

If you do not already own a horse but are contemplating buying one, do give the following facts some careful thought:

> The cost of keeping a horse begins *after* you have purchased him. Such items are:
> 1. **Good quality saddlery.**
> 2. **Feed, hay, buckets, implements, etc.**
> 3. **Shoeing approximately every four to six weeks.**
> 4. **Cost of building a stable, field shelter, repair of fencing, etc.** If you do not own a field you may wish to rent one.
> 5. **Livery.** You may wish your horse to be kept for you by those who are more experienced in these matters. The cost varies; basically you get what you pay for. There are many excellent stables, but also unfortunately still many more where you and your horse may be exploited. When choosing a livery stable look for horses in good condition (if you are unsure then take somebody experienced with you.) Overall tidiness and cleanliness of the yard, stables, tack and feed rooms — these are all pointers to an efficiently run establishment.
> 6. **Veterinary costs.** These can mount up quite alarmingly for even minor ailments. Under this heading I would put regular worming, 'flu and tetanus vaccinations, teeth inspected, etc.
> 7. **Transport.** If you intend taking your horse to shows you will need a trailer or horse box *in good order*. Horses have been known to put their feet through unsafe flooring whilst in transit!) With a trailer you need a vehicle strong enough to pull it safely. Consider also overall maintenance of engine, tyres, bodywork, etc.
> 8. **Insurance** — of horse, transport and yourself — is a must in view of what you stand to lose in the event of accident, theft or damage. Again, companies and policies vary. A good broker can advise you; or go to one of the well established reputable horse specialist companies.

As in all sports, there are "hidden" costs which you must allow for if you wish to enjoy your horse and keep him in the manner he deserves.

Being a horse owner is quite a responsibility, but the rewards often more than outweigh the sacrifices. What price the quality of life?

Part One

GENERAL PRINCIPLES

Frontispiece: The Riding Club Championship, 1972. High Fen Riding Club *Prix-Caprilli* Team — Author centre.

CHAPTER 1

SELECTING YOUR HORSE

SUITABILITY

It is true to say that beauty is in the eye of the beholder, but this can be the downfall of many a would-be horse owner. When setting out to purchase a horse, take an experienced person along with you who knows your capabilities and also what type of horse you are looking for.

Whether you are seeking a horse to ride purely for pleasure or for competitive work, you require a horse that is sound in wind and limb, so it is essential to have a veterinary inspection before you buy your horse.

CONFORMATION

Conformation is the make and shape of the horse. If you are purchasing a horse for show purposes, his conformation must be of the best you can find. However, you are unlikely to find the perfectly formed horse and even if you did, it does not necessarily follow that he will make a good horse.

THE MAIN POINTS TO CONSIDER

The horse should move straight (observe him on the move both being led and ridden). Watch him from the front, sides and rear. The horse should look in proportion, he should be neither too short or too long in his back or neck, though the horse may look an odd shape, if he is being badly ridden or lacking in condition and muscle.

His feet should be well-shaped, the front feet should be a matching pair and neither too narrow or too flat. The hind feet should also be a pair and are slightly narrower than the front. All feet should look strong and healthy and free from cracks. His feet should be level on the ground (pick up the feet to see if the shoes are wearing level). The horse's legs should be straight and free from excessive signs of wear and tear. The horse's head should be small and neat with large eyes and an intelligent outlook.

It may be difficult for the novice to assess a horse's temperament at first sight. Consider the horse's expression, his willingness to do what is asked and his demeanour when being handled. When trying out a horse, with a view to purchase, feel his legs and pick up his feet. If possible saddle him yourself.

AGE

A horse is not fully grown until he is at least six years of age; before this he is mentally and physically immature, his bones are not yet fully formed and ready for any real work. Horses grow and mature at different rates; if poorly developed as a youngster, the horse may never fully build up to his expected size.

If you purchase a horse of any age in poor condition, it may take many months before he is able to cope with any real work. So be prepared to be patient. A horse who is well cared for, intelligently fed and schooled will probably work happily well into his twenties. Although a horse described for veterinary purposes is said to be aged after nine or ten years, this is only because it becomes more difficult to define his exact age after this time. It is not meant to suggest that the horse is getting old. One more point relevant to the horse's age, if you are a novice rider, it is unwise to buy a young horse who knows as little as you do. It is a mistake to think that the novice rider and young horse will learn together, this combination will only lead to problems, particularly for the horse. A novice rider should buy as his first horse, one that has some training and experience of life. This way you will learn from the horse and improve your riding more quickly.

BREED

In the British Isles we have many excellent native breeds of horses, and ponies whose temperaments are generally well suited to schooling. Many of these have been cross-bred to produce horses and ponies of larger or smaller proportions for more specific purposes. When buying a horse try to make sure as far as you possibly can that he is capable of the work you require. If you really like the horse but are unsure whether some defect in his conformation will stand up to hard work, ask the advice of your veterinary surgeon. I have often found that apparent defects of conformation are minimised by schooling and consequent improved muscular development.

SUITABLE SADDLERY

SUITABLE SADDLE

It is most important that the rider be comfortable in his saddle. Some of the rider's problems with position may stem from an incorrectly fitted saddle or one that is the wrong size or shape for the rider. The most useful type of saddle is a general purpose, which as you can see from the

4

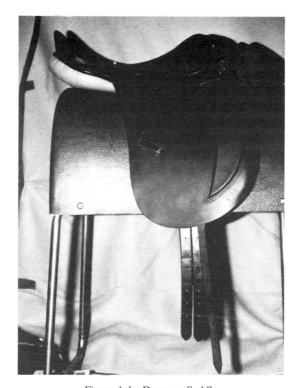

Figure 1-1　Dressage Saddle

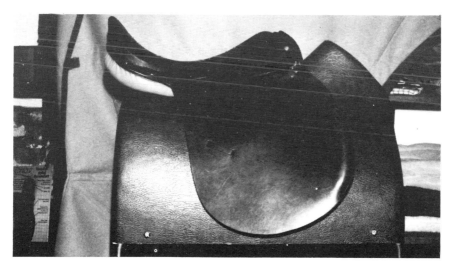

Figure 1-2　General Purpose Saddle

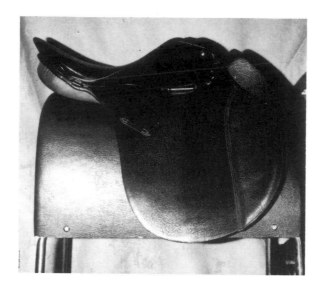

Figure 1-3   Jumping Saddle

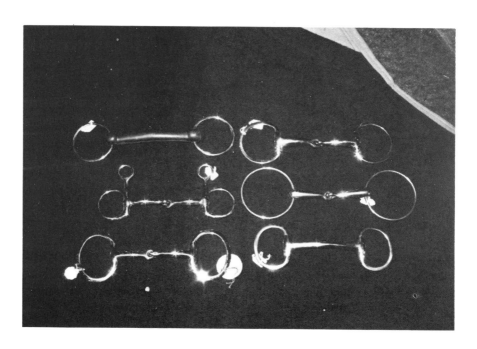

Figure 1-4   Selection of Suitable Snaffle Bits

photographs shown, can be used for jumping as well as hacking and schooling.

The fit of the saddle is most important to the comfort of the horse and correct position of the rider. The saddle must follow the contours of the horse's shoulder and not press down on any part of his spine, it must also be level from pommel to cantle to enable the rider to sit in the deepest part. The deepest part of the saddle should be as close to the horse's centre of gravity as possible. If you are unsure as to the fit or suitability of your saddle, ask an instructor or your local saddler to check for you.

HINTS ON BUYING

There are many makes of saddle on the market, so there is every opportunity to purchase one that fits both you and your horse. Do not be tempted to buy a cheap saddle, particularly at a sale, as there are inferior and even dangerous saddles on the market. Go to a reputable saddler who has a large selection of saddlery. Take your horse along if possible too, so that the saddlery can be fitted on with girth and stirrups. You can then sit or ride on the saddle to make sure it fits you. Make sure you can alter your stirrup lengths and your position in the saddle if you intend to use the saddle for jumping and for flat work. some saddlers will come out to prospective clients and fit saddlery. You can also, if you wish, have a saddle made to measure; this, of course, will cost a little more.

WHICH BIT AND BRIDLE?

I do not intend to go into great detail about bits and biting, as there are suitable publications readily available on this subject. I would, however, like to offer a few suggestions as to the effect your chosen bit and bridles may have on the training of your horse.

There are a great many bits available for the rider to choose from; if you are satisfied with the bit you use on your particular horse, there is no reason to change it. If, however, you are having problems with your horse's mouth when riding, seek expert advice before you decide to change the bit. Most horses go happily in a simple snaffle bridle if correctly fitted and intelligently ridden. There are however occasions when you think you are doing everything correctly and still the horse does not seem to respond in the right manner. Whatever bit or bridle you use on your horse, if he is not comfortable with it or the way in which his rider uses it he will let you know in one of the following ways:

1. Leans on it, takes hold of it or even runs off.

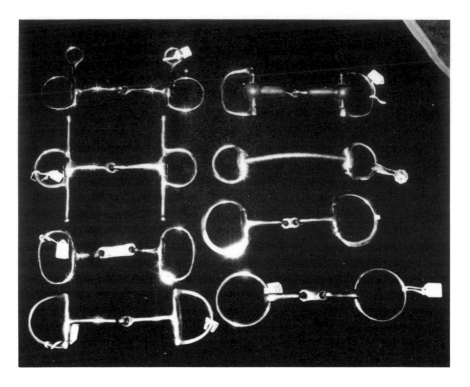

Figure 1-5 Further Selection of Suitable Snaffle Bits

Note: You should study the text on the importance of the tack and equipment making sure that it is appropriate for the horse or pony considering the functional requirements, suitability for the particular horse and purpose; e.g. for shows.

2. Continuously pulls the reins out of his rider's hands.
3. When asked to turn his head and neck in one direction, pulls his head the opposite way.
4. Overbends — tucks his chin in towards his chest and "drops" the bit contact.
5. Raises his head above the point of control and opens his mouth.
6. Crosses his jaw.
7. Lolls his tongue out of the side of his mouth, under or over the bit.
8. Throws his head up and down.
9. May refuse to go forward at all, may rear or run backwards.

Likely Causes of the Horse Evading His Bit —

The Rider Who:
(a) Is not in balance with his horse, either tips too far forward or too far back is unlikely to be able to maintain a steady contact on the horse's mouth or give clear aids.
(b) Uses the bit and reins to keep his own balance; this will cause the horse to become frustrated and try to pull the reins out of the rider's hands.
(c) Has one rein shorter or one hand higher than the other, this over a period of time will make his horse become stiff and one-sided. (See page 89).
(d) Has his arms or wrists too straight or wrists too curved. These do not allow the horse his natural movement of head and neck. The horse will probably show his discomfort by tossing his head up and down. In the extreme case, the horse may refuse to go forward at all and even rear. Hands that fall below the horse's line of contact are likely to have the same effect. These faults also over a period of time will cause an overall tension and stiffness in the horse.
(e) Rides with a slack rein then "pulls" to turn or stop. This rider cannot expect his horse to work in a steady confident manner as he never knows when he is going to get a jab in the mouth.

MOUTH AND TEETH — PROBLEMS

SORE MOUTH

Always check the horse's mouth at the corners of the lips, *also inside* the corners for any signs of the bit chaffing.

A damaged or malformed jaw is difficult to bit comfortably as is a mouth with "bars" that have a sharp ridge to them.

A mouth with a lot of flesh inside the lips or a large tongue may be uncomfortable in certain types of snaffle.

WOLF TEETH

Small extra teeth may appear which, if found in the bit area, will cause discomfort and even severe pain to the horse. These are a common cause of mouth problems.

Sharp molars may also give rise to some discomfort. The horse's mouth should be inspected regularly for any signs of soreness or teeth troubles. Any problems of this nature are a matter for your veterinary surgeon.

INCORRECT BITTING

Too severe a bit, particularly at the hands of a novice, is a likely cause of evasions though any bit may be too severe if misused or incorrectly fitted. If you are unsure which bit you should use in your horse's mouth, start with a plain jointed or unjointed snaffle with a mouthpiece that is neither too thick or too thin. If this seems to cause problems then either:

    (a)   Your riding may be at fault, or

    (b)   the horse has mouth or teeth problems, or

    (c)   the bit may be too narrow or too wide for the horse's mouth, or,

    (d)   it may be fitted too low or too high in the horse's mouth.

I have on many occasions seen bits, particularly snaffles, fitted too low in the horse's mouth by owners who think that if the bit slightly wrinkles the corners of the mouth then it is correct.

The tongue over the bit evasion often begins this way. If, when seated in the saddle, you pick up the rein contact and the checkpiece of the bridle becomes rather slack, then your bit is probably too low in the horse's mouth. There are, of course, occasions when a simple snaffle is uncomfortable for a particular horse, but whatever bit you decide to use on your horse, make sure you are using it for the right reasons. For instance, you may hear a rider state "I cannot stop my horse unless I put him in a pelham" (or whatever). More than likely, the horse is unbalanced with too much weight on his forehand therefore unable to stop himself. The rider should therefore learn more about how his horse works, both mentally and physically, before changing what the horse wears on his head and in his mouth. The rider should learn to interpret

Figure 1-6 Faulty Riding

Top and Bottom: Hands unlevel and below the horse's line of contact. Weight also pressing down on the stirrup irons causing tension behind the horse's withers and loss of forward movement. (See page 9).

Figure 1-7 Rider Correcting Her Position.
Note: The horse is now able to respond to her driving aids.

the movements and expression of his horse's ears, head and mouth before putting extra nosebands, martingales, etc., on.

N. B. There are occasions, however, when a stronger bit or artificial aid may with care be used; i.e. when the safety of a child or adult novice rider must come first. Bits, bridles, nosebands, martingales and artificial reins all seem to take their turn in the fashion stakes. The intelligent rider is one who is seeking to understand truly how to ride and school his horse by his own understanding, not by constant changes of what goes on his horse's head. There are no short cuts to riding and schooling your horse, it is a long road with many wrong turnings, the rider most likely to succeed is the one who does not look for short cuts but for deeper understanding.

CHAPTER 2

MATCHING HORSE AND RIDER

THE RIDER'S POSITION

This is, for our purpose, the **All Purpose Seat**. This position has been developed to assist the rider to sit as close to the horse's centre of gravity as possible thus enabling the horse to carry his own weight and that of his rider as efficiently as possible. At a standstill, the horse's centre of gravity is close behind his elbow in the area of the girth (see Diagram 1 opposite). But on the move, this will shift forward and back depending on the horse's head and neck position, his conformation and other bodily movements related to the standard of horse and rider.

The All Purpose Seat can be adapted to dressage (with a slightly longer stirrup) and to jumping (with a shorter stirrup). The correct position takes time and much hard work to achieve. The more often you ride the easier it should become, but if you have ridden incorrectly for a long period of time, then well established faults may take some time to iron out.

TOWARD ACHIEVING THE CORRECT POSITION

SEAT AND LEGS

The rider should sit in the deepest part of his saddle and be able to feel his weight equally on both pelvic bones. Your shoulders and hips should strive to remain level with each other so that your body is upright (vertical to the ground).

The rider should have the inside of his thigh flat on the saddle. To achieve this take your feet out of the stirrups and stretch the legs as long as possible.

Now take hold of the back of your thigh and roll the knee in, this opens up the hip and allows your whole leg to fall closer to the horse. It also assists the rider to keep his weight evenly on the pelvic bones. The shape of the thigh on the saddle is most important. If you sit on the back of the thigh, as you would if sitting in a chair, you will find it difficult to keep your lower leg in the correct position, so check the upper part first. The inner part of your calf should rest lightly against the horse's side. The ball of your foot (the widest part) sits level on the stirrup iron with toe pointing forward and the ankle joint mobile. The heel should be slightly down. If the heel is raised the rider will be loose

14

DIAGRAM 1 Rider in Balance with Himself and Horse

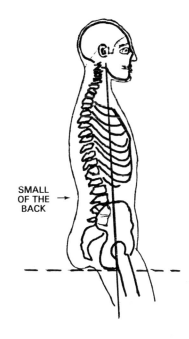

DIAGRAM 2
Showing Skeletal Profile of Rider

Note: It is by exaggerating the normal curve of the small of the back, (by forward and backward movement) the rider may rock the pelvis in order to learn to "follow" the movement of the horse.

It is by "straightening" the spine in the area of the small of the back that the back bracing aids or "brakes" are applied.

SMALL OF THE BACK →

15

in his saddle. If it is too far down the ankle joint is locked, therefore it will not absorb the horse's movement, causing the rider to 'bump' in the saddle. The stirrup leather should be vertical to the ground.

LENGTH OF STIRRUP

As a rough guide, take both feet out of your stirrups and, making sure you are sitting level, allow your legs to hang loosely with ankles relaxed. The base of the stirrup iron should be about level with your ankle bone. This length is for the purpose of everyday riding and schooling and not for jumping. Do not be tempted to ride too long so that the iron keeps slipping and drawing your foot forward, better to ride a little short and work to a correct length. If you are in the right position, there will be flexion in the hip, knee and ankle joints. The motions of these will then help you absorb and follow the movement of the horse. If you have a tendency to "bump" in the saddle, particularly at sitting trot or canter, then it is likely you are not absorbing the movement through these angles of your body.

THE UPPER BODY

You should sit with a normal curve to the spine, do not allow the back to collapse as this will throw you behind the movement of the horse which may upset him or cause setbacks in your schooling. (Diagram 3). The rider who leans too far forward will inhibit the horse from using his shoulders. (Diagram 4). Similarly, the rider who is stiff in his back and sits bolt upright will oppose the forward movement of the horse. (Diagram 5). It is like riding with the brake on and no amount of driving with the leg will overcome this. Keep the back of your neck toward the back of your collar and always look about you and be aware of all that is going on, particularly any distractions which may affect your horse. If riding in company with other horses, be aware of where others are going (as you would if driving a car) and never ride too close behind another horse, particularly a strange one. Also never ever overtake close to a strange horse.

MOTION OF THE PELVIS

This is most important if the rider is to follow the movement of the horse. Sit still yet think about feeling mobile from the waist down. (A good exercise to help feel this movement of the pelvis is to lie on the

16

DIAGRAM 3 Rider with Incorrect Posture

Note:
Shoulders rounded, rider's back collapsed therefore lower leg (below knee) slides forward. The pelvic bones are no longer in contact with the saddle. The rider is out of balance with horse. Arms too straight.

Effect on horse: Rider causes horse to flatten his back therefore raise his head in discomfort and shorten his strides. The horse will become an uncomfortable bumpy ride, he actually feels blocked by his rider's arms and hands.

N.B. Depending on the horse's temperament, if he has to carry himself in this way he will find it almost impossible to "go forward" smoothly. This leads on to all sorts of problems.

17

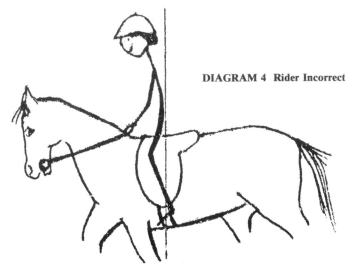

DIAGRAM 4 Rider Incorrect

Note: In front of horse's movement causing hands to drop below horse's line of contact and lower leg to swing back.

Effect on horse: Continual tipping forward of rider will overburden horse's shoulders thus causing him to "tip" forward, also rider's hands will cause horse to resist and throw his head up and down. Lower leg sliding back causes rider to use backward and upward aid thus confusing horse.

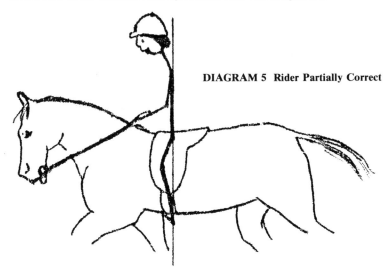

DIAGRAM 5 Rider Partially Correct

Note: Body position basically correct but neck and head poke forward and move excessively. This is caused by rider not absorbing movement through hip and pelvis. Rider will be stiff in his back which will cause muscular strain. This in turn will communicate to horse and cause tension.

18

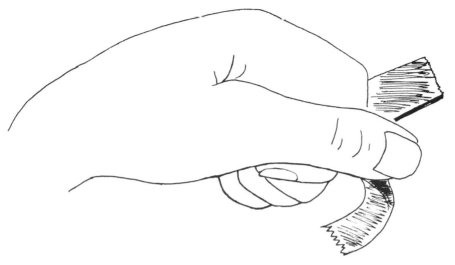

DIAGRAM 6 Correct Wrist

DIAGRAM 7 Incorrect Wrist — too rounded

DIAGRAM 8 Incorrect Wrist (Too straight, fingers open)

floor — knees bent, feet flat on the floor — with one hand under the small of your back and tilt the pelvic girdle up and forward. Keep your shoulders flat on the floor). Now try to feel this rocking motion of the pelvis, keeping the rest of your body still whilst you are riding.

SHOULDERS AND ARMS

Shoulders should be square and relaxed. They should remain level with the horse's shoulders, so as the horse turns or bends (say to the right) your right shoulder should move back and the left one slightly forward.

Common Faults: The rider may drop one shoulder (usually the inside one) on the turn. This will push the rest of the rider's body out of balance and lead to further problems.

Let the upper arm hang naturally with the elbow bent and lying close to your sides. Have a straight line from elbow down through the hand along the rein to the horse's mouth, this gives you a direct contact with the horse's mouth. (Make sure the elbow does not come behind your sides as this will make you and your horse tense.) The whole of the rider's arm should be able to move forward to follow the movement of the horse's head and neck without the rider losing his own balance.

REIN CONTACT: YOUR LINE OF CONTACT
TO THE HORSE'S MOUTH

This may vary according to your horse's standard of training and how he carries his head and neck. If the horse has a fairly high head carriage, then your hands must be carried a little higher than if riding a horse with a lower head carriage. If your hands are allowed to drop below the horse's line of contact, he will toss his head and become unsettled. Never try to pull your horse's head down, he will lower it of his own accord once ridden correctly. Similarly, do not try to follow the movement by moving your hands back and forth.

HANDS

The wrist should be slightly rounded so that your hand will follow the movements of the horse's head and neck naturally. The horse needs to use his head and neck to balance himself, so the rider has to learn to keep a steady "elastic contact on the horse's mouth. If the wrist is straight or bent too much, there will be no elasticity so again the horse will show this by being unsettled in his mouth. (See diagrams 6, 7 & 8).

The rein should pass through the hand between the third and fourth fingers and out over the base of the first finger with the thumb down on the rein to stop slipping. The thumb remains uppermost. If the rein keeps slipping and you have to keep shortening it, this will also upset the horse. You may find that he tugs the reins out of your hands.

From your early riding, you should have become increasingly (sometimes painfully!) aware of the movements your body can make smoothly and those which are seemingly more difficult.

Good riding is about physical and mental awareness. Give some thought to your posture when *not* on a horse. Do you sit, stand, walk with level shoulders and your head straight? Do you know whether your spine remains in its normal curve and your pelvic girdle stays in balance? Are the movements you make when at work or even at rest, rapid or are they slow and smooth and measured? Obviously any postural fault and tensions will still be there when you are on the horse.

Riding is a consistently disconcerting experience. It is the challenge that this represents which makes most of us determined to overcome each set-back and keep on trying to succeed.

THE RIDER'S POSITION ON THE MOVE — WORKING TOWARDS AN INDEPENDENT SEAT

WHAT IS AN INDEPENDENT SEAT?

The rider is trying to attain a supple position in the saddle at all paces by the muscles of his body being totally controlled. You should be able to feel that you can move any part of your body at will without it upsetting your own balance or that of your horse. This is called having an independent seat.

THE RIDER'S POSITION AT WALK

Whilst in walk you have more time to make adjustments in your position. Do ensure that any movements you make in the saddle are done with care. Remember it is your horse's back you are sitting on. The rider should strive to be upright and controlled in the saddle. He should at *all* times be mentally alert whilst riding.

THE POSITION AT TROT

At all times the rider is trying to remain in balance with his horse. At a sitting trot the body remains upright whilst at rising trot, the upper body leans slightly forward to follow the movement of the horse. If you have difficulty maintaining the rising at a regular rhythm, it may be because you are allowing your back to collapse each time you sit in the

Figure 2-1 Incorrect Position

Note: Rider tipped forward sitting on back of thigh therefore lower leg is turned away from horse. This "loose" position has caused the rider to apply incorrect leg aids (backwards and upwards) and drop her rein contact. See the effect on the horse.

Figure 2-2 Position Correcting.

Note: Rider has altered her upper body and changed the hip and thigh position so that the lower leg is now able to "push" the horse forward towards a contact.

saddle, so try to keep the back in its normal curve, bend from the hip and allow the shoulders to lead the rise. Holding a neckstrap or piece of mane will also help.

If you have problems trying to sit to the trot, you may be tipping forward, sitting stiffly or collapsing your back. Either way, your body will be out of balance, therefore unable to absorb the movement. Practise the sitting trot by putting reins and whip in one hand, and holding the front of the saddle with the other. Bring the horse back to walk frequently to correct your position. Remember if you bump about in the saddle, the horse will be suffering as much if not more than you are!

THE POSITION AT CANTER

The canter can be a difficult pace for the novice or inexperienced rider to sit correctly to, particularly if you are riding a short striding or unbalanced horse. It can also be difficult in that you have to try to keep the horse in canter, maintain your balance *and* steer the horse in the right direction. It is best if you can practise the canter on a longer striding animal who is smoother to ride. If you find you are unable to sit down to the canter, it may be as in the trot, you are stiff or allow your back to collapse. (This means that the hip and pelvis do not follow the movement.) Any collapsing of the back will also cause the lower leg to slide forward. This means the rider will have difficulty maintaining his canter aids.

Whilst cantering try:

1. **Keeping the shoulders upright; almost feel as if you are leaning back.**

2. **To prevent shoulders falling forward as this will "block" the horse's own use of his shoulders.**

3. **To feel the mobility of the canter through the pelvic movement.**

4. **Holding the saddle with one hand. This helps you to maintain correct lower leg position, particularly of the outside leg.**

EXERCISES FOR THE RIDER

If you choose to have lunge lessons you will be put through a series of exercises on the horse which help you become supple in the joints and muscles used for riding.

Figure 2-3 Incorrect Canter

Note: Behind the movement, hanging on to horse's mouth, lower leg sliding forward, therefore all aids not "on". Note effect on horse — horse leaning on to forehand his hindlegs unable to propel him forward.

Figure 2-4 Correcting

Note: Rider has altered her body to bring herself in line with horse's balance. Leg aids are now asking horse to bring his hindlegs under. Rein contact much improved.

24

EXERCISES AT THE HALT

Here are a few movements to practise yourself. One word of caution though, do be careful when beginning any form of exercise to build up slowly. No matter what age you are and how easy the exercises seem to be, they will not be of help if you do too much at once, become stiff and have to rest for a few days to recover. Do a few exercises each day so that you gradually become more supple. Take care also if you ride a young, unfit or nervous horse as any sudden shifting of your balance, or leg or arm movements may upset him.

TOUCHING THE TOES

Tie your reins in a knot and let them rest on the horse's neck; if he puts his head down either have an assistant hold him or hold the buckle end of your rein with one hand. If you do a brief exercise session each day, you will probably find he will soon stand still anyway. Raise the right hand and arm straight above the head, reach down to touch the right toe, count two and reach slowly back up again. (I say slowly because most of the exercises will be more beneficial done slowly and correctly.) Repeat twice more. Now do the same exercise with the left arm and hand. To finish, take a deep breath, breathe out slowly and relax. If you find that whilst touching one toe the opposite leg slides back, repeat the exercise and concentrate on the legs remaining in their correct position. Vary this exercise by touching the right toe with the left hand and vice versa or touching both toes with both hands; try not to let your seat slide back or your lower leg slide forward.

SHOULDERS

Many riders become too tense in the neck and shoulders and this will communicate both down your spine and arms to the horse. Lift shoulders up, back, then down. Repeat several times. Turn the head slowly to the right then face front. Repeat exercise to the left. Helps release neck tension. Repeat this exercise several times.

ROTATING ARMS

Again raise the right arm straight above and close to the head and slowly swing the arm backwards and down in a large circle. Keep the arm straight. Pass it close to your head. Repeat three times. Now do the exercises with the left arm.

25

Put both hands on your hips and swing the upper body left twice then right twice. Repeat whole exercise three times. Or swing the upper body side-to-side in the same manner with arms outstretched. Try to maintain the correct leg position and level hips. The above exercises can be done with or without stirrups. If you wish to do them without stirrups, then either remove them from the saddle or cross the irons over. To cross the stirrups so they are out of your way, pull the buckle down from its position until it is well down the saddle flap. Now grasp the whole leather and stirrup iron and lay the iron across the horse's neck with the buckle on the underside and lay it on his opposite shoulder. Twist the remaining leather attached to the stirrup bar until it lays as flat as possible under the skirt. Cross the right stirrup over first, then the left, the reason for this will become obvious if you lose balance and slip off.

ANKLES

Keeping the whole leg still, draw a circle with the toe first in one direction then the other. When the ankle joints begin to ache, relax and drop the toe. If you do have difficulty bending the ankle joint, this exercise can be done whenever you are sitting at home in a chair. Simply cross the right leg over the left and rotate the right ankle as previously described. Change legs and repeat.

BACKS

If you are a back sufferer, as many riders are, then try to go swimming two or three times a week. It will strengthen those supporting muscles.

RIDING WITHOUT STIRRUPS

Work without stirrups may help the rider toward a stronger independent and more effective way of riding. But as with any aspect of riding, this will only be of value if practised correctly. Do not ride without the stirrups if doing so upsets your horse. A young horse particularly, will have insufficient muscle along his back to be "used" in this way. A horse whose muscles are tense and stiff will resent the rider who sits heavily or shifts about on his back. So use your own discretion, do not work totally on yourself at the expense of your horse. If, however, you feel your horse does not mind, then go ahead and practise.

Figure 2-5. Riding Without Stirrups.

Figure 2-6 Irons and Leathers Crossed in front of the Saddle.

Even if you are fairly fit and ride each day, twenty minutes will probably be plenty if this exercise is to be beneficial to your riding. Cross the leathers and irons over in front of the saddle as described previously. Make sure the leathers are well clear of your thigh and the irons far enough down the horse's shoulders so as not to become trapped under the saddle panel. Now, tie your reins in a knot and hold the buckle and in one hand together with the front of the saddle. Allow your other arm to hang straight down loosely with the hand behind your thigh. Correct your whole position and stretch the legs as long as possible (do not worry if the back of your leg is now almost off the saddle flap). Do not "grip" with any part of the leg and whenever you lose your position, bring the horse to walk and begin again. Begin at the walk, then at a slow trot, remember to change direction from time to time. When you feel sufficiently confident, try some changes of pace, walk to trot, trot to canter. The canter is usually easier than the trot without the stirrups, but the transition (change of pace) down from canter to trot may cause you to lose balance. When making any transitions up to a higher pace or down sit well down in the saddle and do not tip forward (hold on as well if you like). Allow the legs to be as long as possible without losing the bend in your knee and ankle. When making turns or circles, make sure you do not lean to the inside of the circle as your seat will slide to the outside and cause your outside leg to slide forward out of place. When turning, keep your weight equal on both pelvic bones and your shoulders level with the horse's.

N.B. If you have persistent problems maintaining your position you may find the jumping position (Chapter 12) will supple you far quicker and with less discomfort to you and your horse.

Good instructors can be of immense help as they will be able to see immediately any problems you may be having and show you best how to correct them. They will have, almost certainly, been through the same frustrations themselves. When you find a good instructor with whom you can work, try to go to them consistently and work on what they tell you. You will get more out of your instructor if you make solid progress as you are, after all, a reflection of their ability to teach. You can concentrate on your riding position during lessons on the lunge. These can be arranged through your instructor or you can contact an approved riding school.

The British Horse Society can supply information on suitable riding establishments. If you really want to ride well, take care where you go, as there are still sub-standard stables about being run by inexperienced people. If you go to one of these, you will actually learn bad habits and could be at risk through riding untrained, badly kept animals.

CHAPTER 3

SAFETY

Safety must be a prime concern, particularly if you ride alone. Take into consideration the following and make sure you:

1. *Always* wear a properly fitted hard hat with a chin strap (elastic will *not* keep your hat on in the event of a fall). Better still, wear a skull cap. A reputable saddler will advise you on this.

2. Wear properly fitting *riding boots*. Long boots made of rubber or leather will give support and a certain amount of protection to calves and ankles.

3. *Jodphurs* are especially designed to allow the rider freedom of movement as well as giving a non-slip surface. Jeans, even stretch ones, are not suitable for the rider who wishes to attain a higher standard of horsemanship.

4. Keep your *arms* covered, especially when jumping, with some sort of sleeves, preferably a jacket. (If the weather is warm a shirt may suffice). Grazes, even from a simple fall, can be extremely painful to arms. (Jackets should always be kept fastened).

5. *Gloves*. There are a variety of gloves available from your saddler. Look for those which are comfortable and have some sort of non-slip palm. Plain woollen ones although inexpensive will cause your hands to slip on the reins, will not be sufficiently warm in winter and will wear out very quickly anyway.

6. *Safety in the area you ride*. Check your schooling area regularly for such hazards as fresh rabbit holes, large stones which have come to the surface; and if you keep your horse in a populated area, watch for litter which could be harmful.

7. *Falling Off* — a subject we like to push to the backs of our minds. Nobody actually likes to fall off but as it is an inevitable part of riding you can lessen the risk of serious injury by learning how to fall. *Main points to consider*:—
   (a) As fear is a considerable contributor to falling off, the rider is likely to be very tense as he hits the ground. It is this tension which will cause you to land heavily.
   (b) If you do fall off there is every chance you may land awkwardly with an arm or leg sticking out, this is how more serious injuries occur.

COMPETITION WEAR

Crash Cap:
For such events as show jumping, showing, etc. (Though some judges may still find crash caps less attractive, if you value your child's head only fit him/ her with the safest headgear).

Jacket:
Black, navy, brown, green, or other colours available. Also various tweeds for casual wear and novice competitions.

Gloves:
Plain leather — again a variety of materials available to suit your needs.

Cane:
Leather covered black or brown. Short cane for decorative (mainly). Use in show classes.

Jodphurs:
Stretch — many colours in the latest machine washable materials available.

Jodphur Boots:
Ankle length, elastic sided, black or brown. Various qualities available.

CASUAL WEAR

Crash Cap:
Topped with a detachable silk. (Various colours available to suit the rest of your outfit).

Waist-coat:
Lightweight, machine washable and comfortable. Many colours and styles available for adults and children.

Gloves:
A variety of styles, colours and materials, many with finger and palm grips.

Jodphurs or Breeches:
Stretch — extremely comfortable, made to fit all shapes and sizes of riders. Available in a variety of colours. Machine washable.

Jumping Whip:
Many variations. Remember for competition use whip should not exceed 30 inches.

Rubber Boots:
Lightweight and comfortable. Washable. Several makes available.

Figure 3-1 Basic Riding Wear. (*Photo: Courtesy Kiln Saddlery*)

Note: This wear may be varied according to the nature of the riding and what the rider can afford. However, for safety and comfort items shown are essential.

(c) If you try to hold onto your horse for fear of losing him consider the consequences of your action. You could damage the horse's mouth; the bridle may come off anyway in your hand. You also run the risk of becoming entangled in the rein and being dragged, or even kicked. Although this may sound rather dramatic, it is realistic to assume you will fall at some point in your riding career. So how do you set about learning to fall with reasonable safety?

You will need the following:

(a) Something close to the ground (soft ground!) to practise technique on. A barrel or bale of straw would do for a start; once you become confident you can progress to the real thing — a pony. Again, once you are sure of yourself, the final stage is your own horse.

(b) You will need an assistant to help you in the initial stages, and later to hold the horse.

(c) Wear proper riding clothes, as previously described, especially a skull cap.

If you have ever observed a jockey fall off you will note how he rolls himself into a ball and, either keeps still if there are other horses about, or rolls away immediately on landing.

It is most important that you remain relaxed when falling off (have you noticed how seldom a baby is hurt when it falls, this is because it knows no fear and is therefore totally relaxed).

PRACTISE YOUR TECHNIQUE

1. Begin by trying a forward roll on the ground. Make sure you fold your arms up to your chest, and that your head is also tucked in. As you roll, keep knees and feet together and take your initial weight on one shoulder. As you go over, remain curled up so that all the joints of your body are mobile and therefore will absorb any jarring. Practise rolling over each shoulder equally, as you may not know which side of the horse you are going to fall from.

2. Having mastered the forward roll in total relaxation, the next step is to do exactly the same thing from your barrel or bale. Once you feel able to fall from this without tension you are ready to try from the back of your pony. Have your assistant hold the pony and first accustom him to your shifting weight by leaning your body over to one side, then the other.

32

Figure 3-2 A Safe Place to Ride

Practise first at a halt, then at a walk. Make sure you do not swing your legs back and knock them against the horse's sides: remember you are trying to maintain your horse's confidence as well as your own. When you feel ready, try the forward roll from the saddle. It is advisable to roll off the first few times from a halt onto a heap of straw or something equally soft.

Follow the same procedure using your own horse.

CHAPTER 4

COMMUNICATION: THE AIDS

INTRODUCTION

The **aids** are the rider's means of communication with his horse. The rider should strive to use "natural aids" as far as possible. These are the voice, legs, seat and back and hands. He must make himself aware of the aids he gives his horse and be sensitive to the way the horse reacts to them. Communication must be two-way between horse and rider, so the rider must learn to recognise when his horse is trying to "talk" to him. Watch the horse's expression when you are riding; his ears, nose and mouth are all expressive and can convey messages to you. Try also to "feel" any tensions in the horse, particularly when asking the horse something new.

THE VOICE

If your horse was trained by conventional methods, he will have begun by being **lunged**. His trainer will have issued commands by use of the voice, supported by the stance of his body and the action of lunge whip.

These voice commands are then used when a rider is put upon the horse to teach the horse the aids. The rider gives light, controlled leg aids whilst the trainer gives the appropriate voice command. For instance, to ask the horse to *trot-on*, the trainer gives the voice command whilst the rider gives light squeezes with the leg. The horse then becomes familiar with the meaning of the aids. These initial stages of the horse's training are best left to those experienced in this work.

USE OF THE VOICE

Though not allowed in dressage competitions, the voice can be of great value during the schooling of your horse. If he is worried or excitable, a soothing voice can be used to calm him. If he is being idle or inattentive, then a sharper tone is required. Use the voice in conjunction with your other natural aids, but as with any of the aids, over repetition will result in the horse becoming bored and unresponsive (rather like listening to a clock ticking, after a while you cease to hear it). Part of the rider's education lies in learning to apply the aids as and when required in such a way that the horse understands perfectly and obeys willingly. The horse *must* also receive much praise as soon as he understands and begins to obey his rider.

LEGS

THE LOWER LEG AS A DRIVING AID

On or near the girth area, keep leg still in its correct position and use in an inward and forward manner (not backwards and upwards raising the heel and knee as this loosens the rider's position in the saddle). See Figures 1-6 and 1-7. The latter aids will confuse the horse. The rider should have the feeling when using his legs, that he is "lifting" the horse's hocks under his body. Use the leg in a series of quick pushes to create impulsion. (This is the energy created by the horse's hindlegs stepping further under his body, thus giving more "spring" to his movement).

AS A CONTROLLING AID

Keep the lower leg closed lightly but steady on the horse's sides when slowing the pace or stopping. The leg holds the horse in position with his hindlegs under his body in preparation for moving on again. The rider's outside leg also controls the quarters if they swing out of line or away from the rider's inside leg.

POSITIONS AND USES OF THE RIDER'S INSIDE AND OUTSIDE LEG

When making a turn or circle or any movement which requires the horse to "bend"* or look to the right, the rider's inside leg is his right. This leg is positioned on or near the area of the girth and creates impulsion by pushing the horse's inside hindleg further under his body. The rider's outside leg is his left leg. This is positioned a few inches further back "behind" the girth and assists in controlling the horse's quarters. When making turns, circles and movements left the aids are reversed.

N.B. Although these leg positions are correct for most of the horse's training, there are occasions when the rider may find it necessary to flout the rules a little. This is further explained in the Schooling Chapters (Part 2 of the book).

PROBLEMS WITH THE USE OF THE LOWER LEG

You may find during the first years of your riding that you experience difficulty in applying your leg aids as and when required. At the walk, you will probably feel you are moving the legs too much whilst at the trot and canter, your legs will not move at all.

*The term "bend" is loosely used as the horse cannot actually bend throughout his whole body. For more information on this subject see Chapter 8.

CONSIDER THE FOLLOWING

1. Try to concentrate on co-ordinating leg and hand aids (described later in this chapter — rein contact).

2. At a rising trot the inexperienced rider uses his legs each time he sits and not when his seat is out of the saddle. Also he will have difficulty in using his legs independently of one another. Try using one leg only keeping the other passive. Try also using the leg or legs three or four times in close succession. Try first at a rising trot, then at a sitting trot.

3. At a canter, try to use your outside leg at each canter stride to help maintain the canter. Consider also whether your inside leg remains on the girth and the outside one behind the girth.

SEAT AND BACK

THE SEAT AND BACK WHEN RIDING FORWARD

The rider's seat is his point of contact through the saddle with his horse. The seat aid may be controlled by the position of the rider's shoulders and the action of his lower back. The seat aid assists in driving the horse forward and is brought into action by the rider feeling as if he is tilting his head and shoulders *slightly* back and allowing his lower back to remain taut but NOT tense. This tilts the pelvis forward and will allow the rider's seat bones to sink into the lowest part of the saddle, closer to his horse. (Do not move about at all in the saddle in an effort to drive the horse with your seat, you will only confuse him, loosen your seat and raise the seat bones off the saddle). Use this aid together with positive leg aids as described, when asking for more speed, impulsion or an upward transition to a higher pace.

THE SEAT AND BACK WHEN SLOWING
DOWN OR STOPPING

When making a transition down or slowing the speed of the pace, keep the lower leg still but definitely on the horse's sides. Then brace the back muscles in the area of your waist as follows:— **Tighten the back (have the feeling that you are momentarily sitting against the movement of the horse) for a count of 1-2, or 1-2-3, repeat and relax the aid until the horse has responded as desired. Use this aid as often as you feel the horse rush or lose his balance.**

36

N.B. If you are unfamiliar with this aid, try the following exercises:
1. Ride the horse in a rising trot which is too fast on a slightly stronger than normal rein contact for about twenty yards or so; now brace **each time you sit** through three or four (or more) sit phases of the rising trot.
2. Count 1-2-3-4 and see how the horse reacts. He should slow down without your having to actively use any rein aid (just maintain a steady contact). If he does not, then practise at the walk first walking on, then slowing down almost to halt, then walk on again. In this case, count 1-2 then release the aid.

Repeat these exercises three or four times and see if the horse feels smoother and more responsive to ride afterwards. Remember also the correct leg aids for riding forward and for slowing down. I find the back bracing aid most useful on horses who fuss and worry about their mouths as you can slow down without actively using your reins by just maintaining steady contact.

N.B. Experiment with the strength of the back bracing. You will find that a young horse, particularly one who is still soft in his back muscles, will be quite sensitive to this aid. If the horse slows down too abruptly or starts throwing his head, then the aids you are using may be too strong. Test the degrees of aid needed at all paces and at varying speeds. Note your horse's reaction.

HALF-HALTS

The back bracing may also be used as a half-halt. Apply this either when the horse feels too strong in your hand or as a warning to the horse that you are about to ask him to do something different. Use it (as described previously) before each change of pace, speed, direction, in fact before any movement you require. This aid is of enormous value. If the horse does not at first show any reaction to the back bracing aids, it is probably because the horse's back muscles are tight and tense. He finds himself unable to respond to you. In this case, you will need to use your voice and rein aids to support the back bracing aids to begin with.

SUMMARY

The frequent and measured use of the back and seat aids will help the rider in the suppling and re-balancing of his horse. Riders who are able to develop and refine this aid will find their riding takes on a new dimension. They will feel capable of riding successfully a greater variety of horses.

HANDS AND ARMS

THE RIDER'S HANDS — EFFECTS OF

The rider's hands holding the reins are largely responsible for the effect the bit has in the horse's mouth. They can encourage or retard the progress of the horse. Whilst discussing the rider's hands, I must also include upper arms, elbows, wrists and fingers as all must "work" together.

UPPER ARMS

The rider's upper arm muscles can tense or relax depending upon the situation. For instance, if the horse is pulling or leans against your hand, tension of the arm muscles will help prevent you from being pulled forward. Absolute control of these muscles is important on a fresh or excitable horse to help calm him. The rider who feels nervous will tend to over-tense these and other muscles of his body which will communicate itself to the horse and in turn make him tense.

ELBOWS

The rider should be very aware of the elbow joint itself which can also affect the mobility of the horse. Elbows should be well oiled and supple to allow the horse to stretch and use his neck. They can however "lock" together with shoulders, upper and lower arms when the horse pulls or leans against the rider.

WRISTS

Can be very mobile (slightly curved); can be stiff (without any inward curve); or be momentarily "locked" (very curved) by the rider. Most important, the wrist must "allow" the natural movements of the horse's neck and head as he needs to use these freely to help maintain or adjust his balance. (See Diagrams 6, 7 and 8, page 19).

FINGERS

The rider must be able to open and shut the fingers at will without gripping the reins or allowing them to slide through his fingers. If you feel that the horse is tense or worried in his mouth, make sure that your fingers are closed and still unless being used as an aid. As a guide, feel that you are holding a ball of wool in your hand, a strand of which is attached to the bit. The rider should make frequent checks on *both* arms

38

and hands and make sure his reins are the same length and his hands are level. Look also at both wrists to see they are correct and held in equal shape. (See Diagrams 6, 7 and 8).

REIN CONTACT

The leg and seat aids (and even the rider's voice) must be able to effectively drive the horse forward before rein contact can be successfully established. Years ago, riders were considered to have "good" or "bad" hands according to how light and still they were able to keep them, though this may not have had anything to do with actual positive contact on their horse's mouth.

As we move on to deeper understanding of the way we ride and school our horses, so we begin to realise that unless the horse is able to happily accept the contact we have on his mouth, we shall have little control. This can lead to difficult, even dangerous situations, particularly when riding in company or out on the busy roads of today. Some riders may feel wary of the amount of contact they have with the horse in case they hurt his mouth. Through his learning process the rider must try to understand and feel the difference between no contact, a good contact, and too strong a contact.

The correct contact is not entirely achieved by the rider having his reins the correct length or his hands in a certain position, but by a positive co-ordination of all his aids. He must drive the horse up to a steady hand which though giving, does not drop if the horse resists against it.

The correct contact you are seeking feels "elastic" and is a significant step forward for the rider once he realises this. The rider who tries to achieve what he thinks is the correct contact by excessive use of his hands is doing himself and his horse a great disservice. The rider's hands must *not* move or niggle the bit about in the horse's mouth in order to make the horse feel "light". The horse *will* accept his rider's hands once he is correctly balanced. (This we will discuss in Part 2). There are no short cuts along the road of correct training. It is a steady, slow progress which is most rewarding for those determined enough to keep going.

REINS

REIN AIDS

The learner rider will be taught very basic aids until the co-ordination of all his aids improves and his riding becomes less hesitant and more natural. Once he is able to establish an "elastic" feeling contact on his horse's mouth, he will find there is a great deal more to the use of the reins than he first thought. The reins in conjunction with the seat, back and legs can generate:

1. **More speed, or less speed.**
2. **Lengthening or shortening the horse's bodily shape and his stride.**
3. **Sideways and backwards movement.**
4. **Transitions from one pace to another or alterations within a pace.**
5. **Turns and circles of varying degrees.**

When using the rein aids remember they are the *last* in any sequence of aids to be applied. The horse *must* be activated by the rider's driving aids first.

TO INCREASE SPEED, IMPULSION, LENGTH OF STRIDE OR MAKE AN UPWARD CHANGE OF PACE

The hands allow as much or little of the above, but can only do so if you have placed the horse on an elastic contact first. So, make sure you push the horse's hindlegs under his body until you have a positive, even feel along both reins to the horse's mouth. Then you can ask the horse to increase, by slight relaxation of the fingers (do not allow the reins to "slip" through your fingers).

TO SLOW DOWN, STOP OR MAKE A DOWNWARD TRANSITION

Making sure the horse is on as steady a contact as possible and using the seat, back and leg aids *first*, the rider may then open and close the fingers of one or both hands, if necessary. Never pull sharply on the reins as this will be painful to the horse and will only result in more resistance. Any rein aids should be applied with subtely and be clear to the horse. Take care to *observe* the horse's reaction to your slowing down aids. Too strong or sudden an aid will cause the horse to resist (resistances are dealt with throughout the book). Personally, I use rein aids only to slow down or make a downward transition if the horse is persistently resisting my back and seat aids or feels very heavy in my hand.

ARTIFICIAL AIDS

There are many aids available on the market today for the rider to use if he so wishes. Most are best left to the hands of experts. Any artificial aid is only intended to make the horse more aware of and understand more clearly the rider's natural aids. Therefore, the artificial aid must not be used on its own but together with the natural aids as far as possible. They should be discontinued as soon as the trainer feels that the horse will respond to the natural aids alone.

WHIPS

DRESSAGE OR SCHOOLING WHIPS

These are available in several lengths. They are designed to enable the rider to use them in the appropriate place without letting go of the rein. This whip is used together with the leg aids, *close* behind the lower leg. Take care to choose a whip that is not too long for you to control as this may upset your horse, thus hindering instead of helping your schooling. The schooling whip should be carried in the hand, with a supple wrist, the whip held across the rider's thigh when not in use. The rider should take care not to pull on the horse's mouth when using the whip, but use it with a sharp "flick" of the wrist when a correction is needed. The whip should never ever be used in temper and only to indicate to the horse that he is not responding to his rider's leg aids.

JUMPING WHIP

Carried when jumping. When used in jumping competitions, must not exceed thirty inches in length and is more stoutly made than the schooling whip. The rider has to transfer both reins into one hand when using this whip.

SPURS

These may be used when schooling on the flat and over jumps. Allowed in jumping and dressage competitions but should only be used by the rider when he is totally able to control the use of his leg. They should fit the rider's boot snugly, with the straps buckled so they face outwards. The spurs should be blunt, curve downwards and be fitted at the back of the rider's boots not below the level of the ankle bone. When used for schooling, they must be applied accurately and in conjunction with, not instead of, the rider's lower leg. When used in dressage, to a higher level, the spur enables the rider to apply a finer aid.

MARTINGALES

These are used to help prevent the horse from throwing or carrying his head above the point of control. If used must be fitted so they allow the horse to use his neck and head to balance himself. A martingale which is too tight is likely to cause the horse to lean upon it as a support. It is also wise to consider that over restriction of the front end of the horse for whatever reason is likely to set up resistance and put considerable strain on the horse's back and limbs. This particularly applies to jumping where the horse needs freedom of his head and neck to shift and balance the rest of his body. The horse cannot be ridden successfully by force or physical strength. Once you have lost your horse's enthusiasm by creating mental and physical tension, you have lost him as a true partner.

THE RIDER'S "FEEL" ON THE HORSE

One of the worries a novice rider has to contend with is the feeling that he does not know what the horse is going to do next. This can be rather unnerving but it is a feeling that disappears in time. This is because the rider gradually becomes more supple, secure and more "with" the movement of the horse and thus becomes more confident. The experienced rider can feel through his body what the horse is about to do before he does it; he can feel any tension or stiffness in any one part of the horse's body or limbs and make that part less stiff or tense. This anticipation and feel is a great asset to the training of the horse as it means that the horse can be asked to do something correctly just as he is about to do it incorrectly.

It also means that the horse who is about to be disobedient will be corrected or distracted smoothly by the rider or trainer before he has even fully planned his tactics. This degree of feel and forward thinking obviously takes time and experience to acquire, but the novice can do much to help himself to this end. As an instance, let us take the horse or pony that shys at one particular place in the field each time he is ridden past it.

This is most annoying for the rider who may punish his horse for this "disobedience" only to find that this makes him worse. The rider then tries to ride straight toward the offending object to show it to the horse only to find that he backs away even more. The rider can avoid all this upset by pretending there is nothing there in the first place. To do this, turn the horse's head and neck away before reaching the offending area. Try to maintain an even contact on both reins. Always ride positively past but not too close to something that the horse may be nervous of or object to, he will soon forget about it because his attention is taken away and focused on what the rider is asking him to do. Therefore, try to anticipate what your horse is going to do. This way you will be concentrating more on the horse than on yourself and your position. This will help towards achieving a partnership with the horse at the same time you are helping yourself towards a "feel". In an ideal "horseworld". ever rider would learn only on a sensible well-schooled horse; he would be taught and supervised by an experienced instructor until he was considered expert enough to train his own horse.

As we do not live in an ideal world where everything has its proper sequence (which on reflection might be rather boring) our world has many novices struggling to train young or unschooled horses/ponies. As a consequence, many riders and would-be trainers find that they have all sorts of problems. As an instructor, I find that many of these "problems" can be solved fairly easily once the rider is helped toward a more thorough understanding of why the horse reacts to situations as he does.

SUMMARY

Though the keen rider is seeking all the time to improve, he must guard against becoming over anxious if his riding position feels less than perfect. Too much concentration on your position will only make you become stiff and mechanical and cause the horse you ride to become the same. To achieve a true harmonious partnership with your horse, you need to strike a balance between working on yourself and working with your horse. The rider who concentrates most on what he can see and feel from his horse (even if there seems very little at first), will become a more calm and natural rider. One of the difficulties for the novice rider is not knowing what it is he is aiming for. He needs a "picture" in his mind. A good instructor can help to create this picture by demonstrating on his pupils' horses or by giving his pupils lessons on a horse of a higher level of training in order that his pupil may "feel" what he is working toward.

THE RIDER'S NERVES

At this point, I would like to add a few words about nerves. Most sensitive people are likely at some time in their riding career to feel hesitant and unsure of themselves. This obviously communicates itself to the horse. So how do you deal with "nerves" when they arise?

Consider the following:

1. Avoid potentially difficult situations where possible. Allow commonsense to prevail. There is no achievement in trying to be brave when you know deep down you are attempting something which is beyond you at that particular point.

   For instance, *do not* jump fences which are too difficult for you as you may make your horse nervous in the process. Do not take your horse out alone if you are unsure of him or yourself.

2. If you are nervous do not get on and ride the horse when you know he is likely to be too fresh. Find someone who can help you or if you know how, then lunge the horse first.

3. If you are a fairly novice rider, you may "worry" about the speed the horse travels. Instead of riding vaguely round and round waiting to see what the horse will do, think positive. Begin at a walk; make the horse turn and circle frequently; make transitions; walk to halt; halt to walk; walk to trot; trot to walk. You will find yourself in control sooner because instead of being merely a passenger, you are riding in a more

definite manner which will build your confidence. As you increase your knowledge, understanding and feel of the horse, so your self-confidence will improve. Riding after a while becomes instinctive.

4. If the actual speed does not concern you but you think your horse may "explode" if you restrict him too much, try the following:

    > Shorten your stirrups to a length suitable for jumping (to give your position greater security) and put the horse almost immediately into canter. Remain in canter (on his best rein first) for three minutes; change direction and establish canter on the other rein again for three minutes. Maintain positive rein contact throughout. Increase the time if your horse is fairly fit or unlikely to settle within six minutes. Ride on as large an area as possible remaining on straight lines as you are less likely to be unseated.

5. Remember the horse will be aware of your nervous state by the smell of your increased adrenalin and also your body tensions. You can distract your horse thereby easing your own tensions by thinking your way round a situation based upon your own capabilities and experience.

As you are able to develop an understanding partnership with your horse, you will find a degree of telepathy will pass between you. Riding is a great leveller too. If you become overconfident and try to push your horse too far, you will find he will "switch off" and will leave you feeling rather humble. It is about self-awareness, self-discipline, knowing your own limitations; but also being unafraid to push yourself!

Part Two

PRACTICAL RIDING

CHAPTER 5

SCHOOLING I

WHY SCHOOL YOUR HORSE?

A well-schooled horse will be happy in himself and a joy to ride, so why do many of our horses not receive their basic education? Do we have so little time to spare? The pace of life today seems to leave little time to reflect and consider our actions, to decide if we are on the right track. Many riders and owners of horses today seem to want instant results. This is so sad as it takes away the excitement and feeling of greater achievement as our horses improve entirely by our own efforts.

The basic training of the horse is important for several reasons now discussed.

SAFETY

The unschooled horse or pony is a liability to itself and its rider. On the road, with the ever increasing volume of traffic, it is vital that the horse is obedient to its rider in all situations. Children especially should not be allowed to ride unaccompanied on the road, neither should novice adults. (If you have problems controlling your horse wherever you ride him, *do* seek professional help).

SOUNDNESS

For the horse to remain sound in his wind (lungs), heart and limbs, he needs to be sufficiently fit for the work required of him. A horse who is unfit and/or unschooled will suffer much strain and concussion to the whole of his body. He must be systematically and steadily built-up, both in stamina and in muscle for the work the rider intends.

It is unreasonable and ignorant of the rider to leave his horse without work (either stabled or in the field) during the week, then expect him to do several hours at the weekend. Any damage may not become apparent immediately but over a period of weeks months or years, continuous strain will cause outward or internal damage.

PERSISTENT PROBLEMS

To the experienced person many problems during the training or re-training of a horse are mere hiccoughs. To the novice, however, many simple mistakes can lead to seemingly insurmountable problems. If you do have persistent troubles of any description with your horse, do seek professional help. It could save you hours of worry and may be solved within a short space of time.

SO WHY DO PROBLEMS OCCUR?

Lack of Understanding

I am always amazed at how tolerant horses are. They seem to put up with the most incredible amount of stupidity on the part of us humans. Many bad habits are caused by the way we treat our horses. At all times, whether riding or handling your horse, try to be most aware of how the horse is feeling. Learn to look, really look, at him. Get to know his character, watch his reactions when he is with other horses. How does he behave in new situations or to a different rider? Learn to really read his expressions, feel his every tension and find out how you can best help him, not bully him through situations.

Let us consider the rider.

The Passenger Rider

The rider who is passive, who just sits on his horse giving vague aids is as damaging as the rough rider who pulls the reins to turn or stop and kicks to make the horse go. Either way, the horse will be confused and show this in a variety of ways, according to his temperament and the situation. He will learn bad habits as quickly as he will absorb good ones. Most problems occur because riders do not understand the effect their body and its actions has on the horse. A rider who really wants to improve, will strive to increase his own understanding of himself as well as his horse. Many problems can be related to the horse's earliest experiences with humans. These are likely to have a lasting effect on the way he relates to us.

A LITTLE UNDERSTANDING

In order to school the horse successfully, you need to understand the way in which the horse carries himself and about his mental attitudes.

The horse is by nature a shy and sensitive animal whose first instinct is to run from situations which frighten him or he cannot understand. He has a strong herd instinct so feels safer when he is with his friends than all alone. He has little reasoning power, so if you need to correct him for some misdemeanour, you must do so instantly or he will not be able to work out why he has been punished. The horse learns by the use of his memory, which means he will retain the bad as well as the good

50

experiences in his life. The rider or trainer must therefore take care to avoid potentially difficult situations where possible.

The horse in his natural habitat spends much of his time with his head down, grazing: this necessitates his centre of balance being well forward. Add to this the weight of a rider and saddle on his back, a bridle on his head, and you increase this tendency to "lean forward". The horse in his early stages of training has to learn to rebalance himself to accommodate the extra weight. The rider, therefore, has to learn how to assist the horse through this process if he wishes to have a pleasurable and useful animal to ride.

LACK OF CONFIDENCE

More horses lack self-confidence than we realize; just because *we* know where we are going or what we are intending to ask the horse, it does not follow that he will co-operate with enthusiasm and alacrity. Horses which lack in confidence and boldness are often ridden with the most passivity. This may seem odd, but horses have a strong herd instinct and most desire to have a "boss" to be led by.

The rider who is able to think ahead, and ride positively, will inspire the most confidence in his horse.

Horses show lack of confidence in many ways; for instance, shying and "spooking" at innocent objects, being nervous in traffic or not liking to be ridden without the company of other horses.

All these are often labelled as naughtiness. The horse gathers confidence from the consistency of his rider and from knowing how his rider behaves in all situations.

THE HORSE'S OUTLINE

The horse may be virtually any age to begin his basic training, though a young horse will be less "set" in his ways both mentally and physically. Do not think if your horse is already in his "teens" that he is too stiff to improve. On the contrary, you will help to slow the ageing process in his limbs by suppling and re-balancing him. It can be just as rewarding an experience schooling an older horse as a younger one. In the following chapters I give you some thoughts and ideas to help you to find for yourself what is or is not correct.

Observe the diagrams of the shape of the horse during the whole of his training. Look at the topline (from his ears to his tail along his spine). During his early training the horse may appear to be short in the neck and longer behind the saddle. This is because his weight is too much on his forehand. If and when his balance alters you will notice a

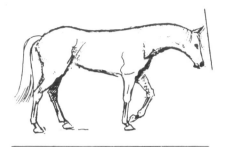

DIAGRAM 9

Outline as it should be in the early stages; long and low allowing muscle to develop which enables the horse to carry himself and the weight of his rider with greater ease.

DIAGRAM 10

Improving balance, building muscle. Shifting towards quarters. Outline shortening slightly.

DIAGRAM 11

Towards the end of the horse's basic training, his topline should be well covered in muscle. His whole body should take on a "rounded" look with an arched neck and relaxed jaw. The horse at this stage is said to be on the bit.

DIAGRAM 12

The ultimate: Horse working in collection, horse's quarters lower, hindlegs take a greater portion of horse's balance.

Figure 5-1 The Shape of the Horse (Diagrams 9—12)

considerable change in his overall shape. The young horse whose quarters are higher than his forehead (because he is still growing) will be unbalanced whilst carrying his rider until he has grown to his full height.

STAGES OF BASIC TRAINING

The basic training as described in this book travels through three stages.

1. Working towards the bit. (Diagram 9)
2. Accepting the bit. (Diagram 10)
3. On the bit. (Diagram 11)

Until the horse has reached the third stage — that of being truly on the bit — his subsequent more advanced training will be at the very least, disappointing. Many promising horses are described as being limited in capabilities simply because their basic training has not been thorough enough.

Some obvious signs of this are:—

(a) Inability to remain straight throughout all the basic paces and during transitions.

(b) Constant changes in outline and a generally unsettled state of working.

(c) No real sign of alterations of pace, particularly where extensions are requested.

(d) Inconsistencies in performance. Horse works better some days than others.

(e) Unlevel pace; sometimes the horse even looks slightly lame.

Often the muscle development along one side of the horse's body is less mature. This is usually caused by some fault in the way he is ridden; i.e. unequal contact, or rider sitting unlevel.

General Appearance: Inadequate muscular build-up for the amount of work the horse is supposed to have done.

Result: Short "stiff" looking mechanical paces.

N.B. I have not marked the stages of training in this book as these cannot have a definitive beginning or end. They of necessity interlock and overlap depending upon which aspects of training each horse and rider finds easier. It is only through experience that you will acquire an "eye" for the progression of yourself and your horse.

MONITORING PROGRESS

The following descriptions of the stages the horse's basic training should pass through are intended to assist you in monitoring your horse's progress.

Stage One: Towards the Bit This is the first stage. The horse alters his head and neck position quite a lot during this time as he lacks muscle and may still be growing. (See diagram 9 — horse's outline). If the rider is quite novice his reactions will be slower and so the horse will progress at a slower rate. Either way do not worry as the horse needs time to adjust to co-ordinating himself, his tack and a rider. There should be moments (they may only be fleeting or may last four or five strides) when the horse lowers his head, stretches his neck, takes an elastic contact and feels more springy throughout. If you are at this stage and experience this then you are on the right road.

General Appearance Some good moments inspire hope in the rider, though much of the time the horse will alter his balance, speed and outline.

Stage Two: Accepting the Bit The horse develops sufficient muscle, particularly in the area in front of the withers and along his back to his quarters, to carry his load. He begins to work with greater consistency. The head and neck are able to become steadier, and his attention is focused more upon his rider than on outside influences. There may even be moments when he feels to be on the bit.

General Appearance The horse looks bigger, more confident, and covers the ground in a more positive and consistent manner. The outline should still be long and low. (See diagram 10).

Stage Three: On the Bit The ultimate of this early training cannot be forced. The horse at this stage feels absolutely incredible. It is a feeling you will never forget once you have experienced it. If you have never ridden a horse at this stage it is very difficult to know whether your training is heading in the right direction. This, of course, is what riding is all about. Striving to find out what lies around the next corner, no sooner do you think you have arrived than you are driven onto the next, and so on.

The horse on the bit is breathtaking to watch; he stands out in a crowd. He may not rate much notice when at rest but on the move has a presence that is exciting to watch. Here I am not talking about breeding, but the confidence attained by his early correct schooling. To those who do not know what I am talking about, here I say *"persevere* and you will know".

The muscle development by this time is most obvious. (See diagram 11). The horse takes on a "rounded" appearance. His topline (from ears to tail) looks well padded. The neck and shoulders should have developed significantly and there should be no sign of tendency to ewe neck or excessively straight shoulders. He carries himself in a constant outline and is able to shorten and lengthen throughout his body. His work is even on both reins and his manner is one of smiling confidence — ears flicking back and forth and flopping sideways a little as he listens in a calm easy manner to his rider. The work he should be doing well by this time is outlined in the schooling chapters of this book. The rider should feel that his aids are applied and received in a fine, almost telepathic, way.

N.B. It is important to remember throughout your horse's (and your own) training that whenever you encounter a problem, however small, stop and think. Try to work out the cause, then eliminate the cause not the apparent problem. Never be afraid to backtrack your horse's training, then work up again. Do not doggedly force an issue; you will almost certainly fail in the long run, if not at once. Your horse will not forget what he has learnt, however long a break he has.

STRUCTURE

The horse's structure and how it works at all paces is a vast subject and one well worth studying. For those who wish to train the horse and rider successfully as a career, a deeper understanding of the physical and mental capabilities of both is most important.

However, in order that the reader of this book may understand the following chapters, I have put together a few facts relating to the horse's movement during the basic training process.

HEAD AND NECK

The horse's head and neck, when raised of his own accord, transfers his balance toward his quarters. When lowered, sends his balance further forward.

Comment

In learning to ride the horse on *his* correct contact, his head and neck remain at a suitable level for his state of muscular development. Some riders try to position the horse's head and neck in what they think looks correct. Unfortunately, this only upsets the horse's natural balance and *limits* his potential.

SHOULDERS AND FORELEGS

The shoulder blades are attached to the horse's trunk by muscle and ligaments (not by bone) and are able to move freely over the ribcage which lays beneath. The forelegs are capable of moving forward and sideways. They are able to move away from and closer in to the horse's body. The main body of the horse, the trunk, consists of the thorax at the front and the abdomen at the rear. The thorax is held by muscle between the forelegs but the abdomen by bone at the hindlimbs. The forehand of the horse then has a greater range of movement than the quarters. The muscular control in the area of the thorax also assists in altering the horse's balance either back or forward or from one side to the other.

SPINAL COLUMN

There are still those who think that the horse is able to bend his spine and round his back in a convex or lateral shape. The spine of the horse has only very little flexibility so these movements are not entirely possible. The horse manages to compensate for this inflexibility by using the whole of his body in co-ordination. It is this co-ordination that gives an illusion of the horse bending his whole body on the move. The joints of stifle and hock with their all important muscles, provide the main propulsive force from behind.

SUMMARY

The forward impetus comes from the activation of the hind limbs of the horse but it is in understanding how we may channel this through the forehand so that the horse may use his whole body throughout all his work.

CHAPTER 6

SCHOOLING II

HOW MUCH SCHOOLING?

In the following chapters I deal in greater detail with the basic training of the horse, including information on what to do when your horse does not respond in the way you expect.

The early stages of the horse's training may take anything from a few weeks to many months depending on the following:

1. The age, maturity, fitness and temperament of the horse.
2. The horse's previous training or lack of it.
3. The experience, temperament and fitness of the rider, and
4. The time the rider is prepared or is able to put in.

The rider should learn to use his common sense to decide how little or how much work his horse can cope with. A *young horse* of three to five years of age will absorb more if schooled for short periods during his first years of training. He tires easily and finds concentration rather difficult. I find that one or two half-hour schooling sessions per day, three or four days per week are ample for a youngster. He should also be taken for interesting rides out, whenever possible. These should be in the company of a more experienced horse to begin with.

Every eight weeks or so I like to omit any concentrated schooling for a couple of weeks and either just hack out quietly or turn him out each day to "unwind". I find that the horse will then come back to schooling quite refreshed (he will not forget what he has learnt), and have also made sure I do not get carried away and ask too much of him all at once. The rider should also try to recognise when he or his horse need a "break". If you come to a point where your schooling is not going right, leave it for a week or two. If, when you start again, the same problem or frustrations are still there, then seek help.

THE OLDER HORSE

Once the horse is over the age of six, he becomes physically and mentally more mature (though he may still have psychological worries which make him seem "babyish"). He should now be able to cope with a more demanding work routine but the rider should remember that too much schooling will only make the horse bored and mechanical.

Decide first of all what your aims are in riding. Maybe you are a comparatively new owner and are unsure what you and your horse are capable of. There are various possibilities open to riders. You may just enjoy hacking around the roads, bridleways and countryside, whatever is available in your area, etc., or join a Riding or Pony Club who offer activities for all standards of riders. If you wish to become a member of a club do not be put off by thinking you are not good enough. There are "get togethers" and events for the very novice as well as for the more experienced riders. You may, of course, be very competitive-minded and purchase your horse with specific types of competitions in mind.

BE CONSISTENT

The horse thrives on a regular routine and is a great "worrier" though he may not show it outwardly. It is therefore important that just as the horse knows the order of things in his stable routine, he must also know what to expect of the rider. Many horses these days have to fit in around our lifestyle; there is a tendency, however unwittingly, for us to "use" our horses. The owner/rider should decide which days he is going to ride his horse, for how long, and what sort of work he is going to do.

TYPE OF WORK ENCOMPASSED DURING
THE BASIC TRAINING

Your weekly routine may encompass the following:

Hacking
Take your horse out for steady but active rides (1—1½ hours about three times per week will keep the horse in reasonable condition). Vary the routes where possible and avoid prolonged trotting on the roads which will cause undue concussion to the horse's limbs. Walking (active but unhurried) is beneficial for strengthening and building muscles. Slow canter work (never on the road) will also assist in the physical and mental stamina fitness of your horse.

Flat Work
This is his serious (but should not be boring) school work. It is done in an arena. If you do not have your own or access to one, then make one for yourself (see following page).

School your horse two, three or four times a week, depending upon how advanced horse and rider are and whether you are working towards a competition. Half to three quarters of an hour's concentrated work is usually plenty for most horses.

Lungeing
Lungeing is also an integral part of the horse's training. It is beneficial

also for the rider/trainer as it will help him to monitor his horse's progress (or otherwise!) from the ground. (See Chapter 7).

Athletic Jumping (see Chapter 12)

Useful whether you intend entering competitions or for the sake of the horse's all round education. It will also help improve the partnership between you.

This type of jumping should be fun as well as educational. Athletic jumping involves the placing of a series of poles and obstacles at varying distances apart. The object of these jumping exercises is to improve the athletic ability of the horse and to teach the rider the feel of shortening and lengthening the horse's stride and therefore ride him in a more positive and accurate manner.

N.B. The inexperienced should learn the correct distance between poles and obstacles for his horse (from an instructor and by reading books on the subject). When you know the actual length of your horse's stride and can negotiate straightforward poles and obstacles confidently, you can then experiment with slightly shortened or lengthened distances but do not attempt anything you are unsure of without the help of someone who knows about this subject.

SCHOOLING IN A FIELD OR ARENA

If you wish to school your horse accurately you must have a set area as a visual guide. You may think you ride really straight lines and truly round circles in a field at home, but the real test comes when riding in a confined space, such as a small jumping ring or a dressage arena, where you are likely to find that the horse does not perform nearly as well.

Schooling does not mean hours of time spent boring your horse and yourself by wearing a circular or rectangular "track" in your field; quite the contrary. To do half an hour's concentrated work in an arena will do more good for rider and horse than several hours vague work in an open space.

If you do not have access to a properly constructed arena, then set one out for yourself as follows:

1. A level surface size approximately 20m × 40m. (This is the arena size for dressage competitions at the earlier levels).
2. Cans (or something to paint letters on) set out as shown in the diagram.
3. Painted white boards pegged into the ground as a surround (not essential, but will help you to riding the movements with greater precision). You can also, if you wish, mow a track or mark the centre line with chalk.

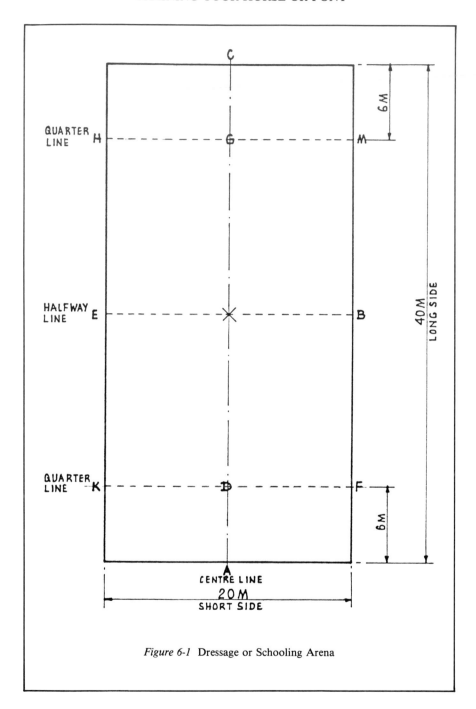

Figure 6-1 Dressage or Schooling Arena

DRESSAGE

On the following page, you will find diagrams of school movements you can make whilst schooling your horse. You will see there are many different movements possible to supple your horse, increase the obedience and accuracy in his paces. Make frequent changes of direction using the movements shown and ride at whatever pace you feel you and your horse are capable of.

SCHOOL MOVEMENTS

Observe the diagrams of various schooling exercises to use throughout the early training of your horse:

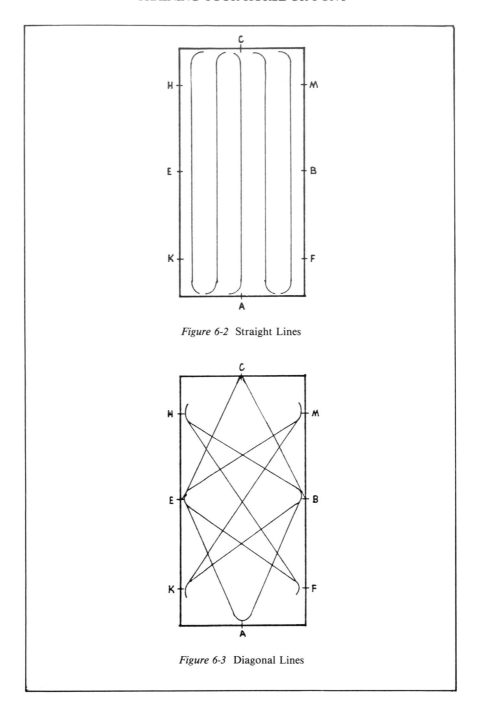

Figure 6-2 Straight Lines

Figure 6-3 Diagonal Lines

Fig. 6-2—Straight Lines: When riding straight lines look at the point you are aiming for. Do not make straight lines only on the centre line or on the track. Try those in diagram.

Suggested Paces: Walk, trot and canter (remember to trot and change canter if you intend changing rein).

Fig. 6-3 — Diagonal Lines: From quarter marker to quarter marker which will give you a change of direction, do in walk, trot and canter. If in canter, come back to trot or walk for a few strides (called simple change of leg through trot) and change canter lead. Diagonal lines can also be ridden in walk and trot from A to B or E, C to B or E. From X to each quarter marker. From B to H or K. From E to M or F. Vice versa where practicable.

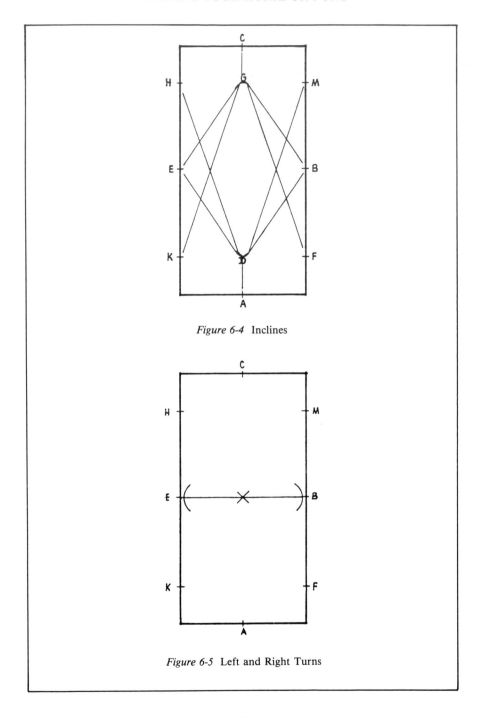

Figure 6-4 Inclines

Figure 6-5 Left and Right Turns

Fig. 6-4—Inclines: Ride up the centre line from A to D. Incline toward E, H, B or M. Down centre line from C to G and incline across the school toward B, F, E or K.

Suggested Paces: Walk, trot and canter.

Fig. 6-5—Left and Right Turns: E turn left at B turn left, E turn left, B turn right, B turn left, E turn right — B turn right, E turn right — B right, E left.

Suggested Paces: Walk and trot. Do canter, through to trot at X but only when canter and correct bends in trot are fairly good.

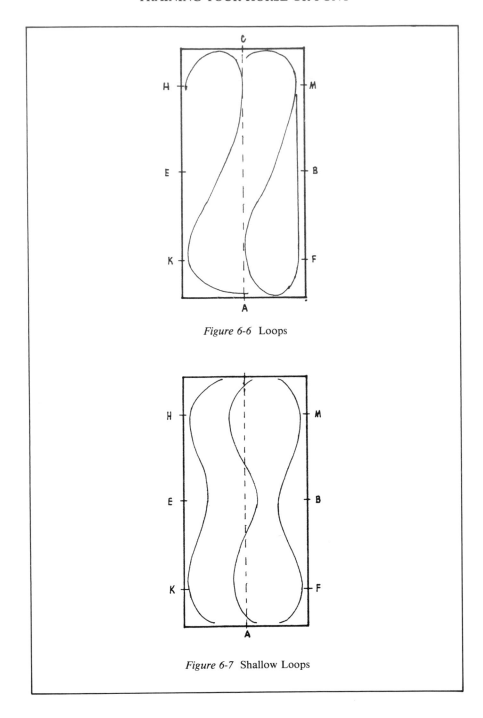

Figure 6-6 Loops

Figure 6-7 Shallow Loops

Fig.6-6—Loops: From each quarter marker ride a curve onto the centre line. On touching centre line ride towards a quarter marker.

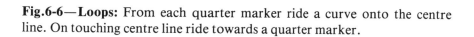

Fig. 6-7—Shallow Loops: 3—5 metres using the wall or centre line as a guide.

Suggested Paces: Walk, trot and *eventually canter.*

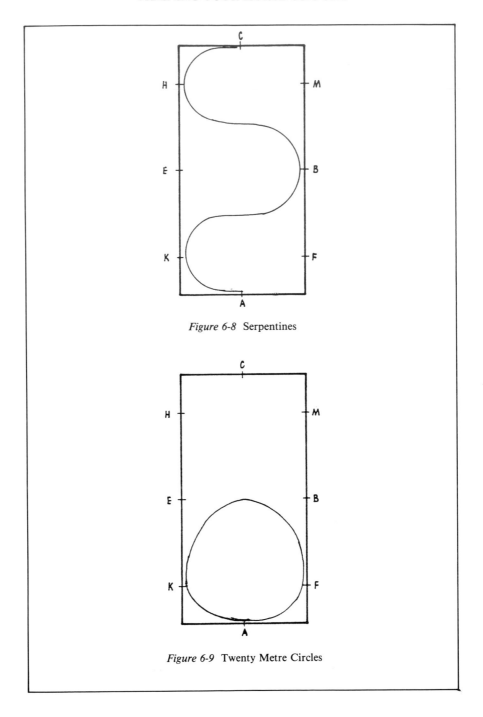

Figure 6-8 Serpentines

Figure 6-9 Twenty Metre Circles

Fig. 6-8—Serpentines: Make three or four even loops; begin at C or A, ride from one long side straight across the arena to the other.

Suggested Paces: Walk and trot. Work on loops being of good shape making the changes of bend good. Do in canter only when you have a well-established canter and can make smooth changes of leg, through trot or even walk.

Fig. 6-9 — Twenty Metre Circles: Begin and finish at same marker either A, C, B or E.

Suggested Paces: Walk, trot and canter.

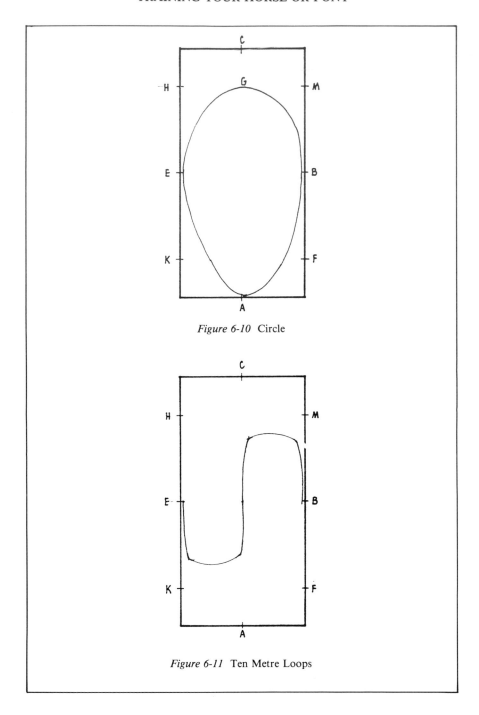

Figure 6-10 Circle

Figure 6-11 Ten Metre Loops

Fig. 6-10 — Circle: Taking in three-quarters of the area.

Fig. 6-11 — Ten Metre Loops: B loops 10m onto X ride straight along centre line, loop left 10m to E or vice versa.

Suggested Paces: Mainly walk, keep loops even shape, walk of even rhythm. Trot when impulsion and rhythm is good and changes of direction are smooth.

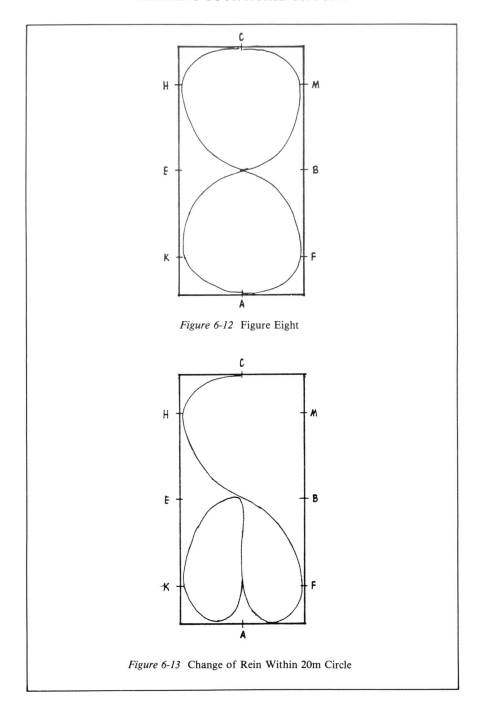

Figure 6-12 Figure Eight

Figure 6-13 Change of Rein Within 20m Circle

Fig. 6-12 — Figure Eight: Should go close to each quarter marker, also C and A ride in walk, trot and canter, pass through X. Remember to change canter lead through trot or walk.

Fig. 6-13—Change of Rein Within 20m Circle: In walk or trot change direction either on centre line or diagonally, and

Change of Rein Out of Circle: Ride in walk, trot and canter.

N.B. Why not try to put together some of the movements shown to make your own test. Ride the test one day then leave it for a couple of weeks and note the improvements (hopefully!). Do not ride often through the same sequence of movements as the horse will very quickly remember and begin to anticipate the next movements instead of attending to his rider.

For those who wish to compete in *prix caprilli* or dressage tests, write to the British Horse Society (address at beginning of book) for test sheets and information on competitions.

CHAPTER 7

LUNGEING THE HORSE

INTRODUCTION

To lunge correctly and with feel is as much an art as is good riding. It is not merely a means to wear the horse out by sending him round and round in a vague sort of circle. On the contrary, lungeing should be a positive way of assessing and improving your horse's paces and of developing a partnership between you.

The trainer/rider should lunge his horse at regular intervals throughout his training to study the improvement (or otherwise!). The lunge is also a useful means of observing and rectifying problems that you may have trouble solving from "on top".

WHERE TO LUNGE

Ideally an enclosed area without too many distractions will make the job easier, particularly for the novice handler. If, however, you do not have a small (20 × 40 metre) arena already fenced then either:

1. construct one, or
2. put up a makeshift but strong looking one. For this you can use jump stands and poles, or even rope off an area in a corner of your paddock. Make sure, if you do this, that the materials you use are not likely to confuse or injure the horse in the event of him getting loose.

SOME DO'S AND DON'TS

DO NOT:

1. Lunge the horse in a large open space if you or your horse are inexperienced.
2. Lunge the horse in the furthest corner of the field away from his friends or the gate. Many horses spend their time focusing upon the field entrance and this can make any form of schooling difficult. Instead, make an area close to the gate where he can perhaps see his friends, or at least know he is near home.
3. Lunge on uneven, sloping or holey ground. Make sure also that there are no stones, lumps or bumps to upset his paces.

DIAGRAM 13 Rider on the Lunge

Note: To lunge correctly and with ''feel'' is as much an art as is good riding.

4. Lunge where there are jumps or loose horses which are likely to distract or cause problems.
5. Canter your horse on the lunge unless you have sufficient experience to know what the horse can cope with — i.e., do you know what size circle or area he can comfortably maintain a truly forward going even rhythm? Of course, if you have a horse who is fresh and canters off at the start of the lungeing session, you will not wish to cause an argument by attempting to slow him down immediately. As it is difficult to steady a lively horse anyway, give him a few minutes to get the high spirits out of his system. Make sure you give him sufficient space (a good 20 metres) and keep his head towards you. This ensures you do not either receive a kick or lose the horse entirely.
6. Use rough or confusing aids such as (1) waving your whip in the air, or (2) walking about too much or (3) a loose rein contact.

DO:

1. Lunge the horse equally in both directions if you wish him to become supple on both sides of his body and level in his paces. Begin with five minutes on each rein increasing gradually to not more than fifteen minutes on each rein.
2. Have the correct equipment and know how to fit it. Ask someone who is experienced in lungeing; or ask your local saddler.
3. Have help if you have little or no lungeing experience. You could save yourself from getting into quite a muddle.
4. Know what size a 15 or 20 metre circle is. If you are unsure, then measure one. Do not guess.

SUITABLE TACK FOR LUNGEING

CAVESSON

If you are to lunge your horse with accuracy and actually improve his paces, then you must have a correctly fitted cavesson. This may be made from leather or washable nylon.

N.B. If you decide to purchase a second-hand cavesson, particularly from an auction sale because it may be less expensive, remember, you are likely to get what you pay for!

LUNGE LINE

Choose one that is long (over twenty feet) and made from webbing (nylon will slip even if you wear leather-palm gloves).

LUNGE WHIP

Various types are available. Choose one which feels most comfortable in your hand, and is long enough to reach the horse if necessary.

SIDE REINS

These are optional. There are several types on the market. Some have elastic or stretchy rubber inserted which "take a play" on the horse's mouth if he resists. The problem with these is they are likely to allow, even encourage, the horse to drop behind the bit. To the inexperienced eye these side reins may give an illusion of correct carriage in the horse's head and neck. A pair of plain leather side reins will give the clearest indication of progress of the horse. If you are unsure of the side reins, begin with them fairly loose and gradually shorten them. (See Figs. 7-1/2). Your horse should still be able to move his nose well in front of the vertical, also to stretch his head and neck down. Make sure your side reins are of equal length. NEVER shorten the inside one to achieve a correct bend. This will only cause the horse to shift his balance and weight and tense the very muscles you seek to supple.

N.B. On a saddle the side reins should slot between the first or second girth strap and the panel. Most importantly the side rein should be anchored above the buckle guards or they will slide down and cause the horse to resist. Do not use when jumping. Never lead your horse with the side reins fastened. If he does become excited he could overbalance or damage his mouth due to the unnatural restriction that he feels. NEVER fit your side reins so tight as to force the horse to arch his neck. This also will create tension and inhibit free forward movement.

ROLLER OR SADDLE

If you are intending to ride your horse immediately after lungeing him then it may be as well to put the saddle and bridle on to start with. In this case, take the noseband off the bridle as it will be in the way of the cavesson. Take the stirrup irons and leathers off the saddle, or run the irons up the leathers and fold the ends of the leathers up. This will prevent the irons from slipping down and banging against his sides.

You can, of course, use a roller instead. If you do, then make sure it fits snugly, will not move about whilst you are lungeing, and is of good quality. Check also that the roller has rings suitably placed for the side reins to be attached.

Figure 7-1 Lungeing With Faults

Note:

Here the handler is slightly in advance of the horse. The rein contact is slack resulting in loss of forward movement.

Figure 7-2 Lungeing Correctly

Note:

The handler is now better placed in relation to the horse. The rein contact is much improved. Note the difference in the length of stride.

79

BOOTS

If you value your horse's legs then fit him with some form of protection. There are all sorts of boots available. Whatever you choose, make sure the fetlock joints are covered. Some horses are inclined to knock the opposite coronet with the inside edge of the shoe. In this case, overreach boots are most useful.

DRESS OF THE HANDLER

Here common sense should prevail. Obviously, if you intend to ride you will be correctly dressed for this. If, however, you intend only to lunge then make sure you have on sensible footwear, comfortable non-flappable clothing and — most important — gloves with a nonslip palm.

THE PURPOSE OF LUNGEING

To lunge the horse correctly you have to learn how to send him into a steady rein contact, as you would when riding. To learn when it is permissible to walk with the horse, and when to stand still.

When lungeing a young or unbalanced horse you need to move about a certain amount or the horse will feel too restrained and will not respond readily to your forward driving aids. As the horse improves you will be able to stand in one place, and ultimately he will be able to sustain his paces to the extent of remaining on a true circle. Do not expect to achieve this in a few days or weeks, it is likely to take some months.

POSITION OF THE HANDLER

Have the feeling of forming a triangular shape. The horse's head, the lunge line, and your hand form one side. The whip pointed towards the haunches forms the other. The horse forms the base of this triangle, and your own body the point. When lungeing to the left, have the lunge rein looped smoothly (never twisted, wrapped or muddled) in your left hand. You should be able to lengthen or shorten the line (and therefore the size of the circle) easily without interfering with the horse's paces. Your body should remain upright, even slightly tilted back if the horse is heavy in your hand. Never lean forward as this will weaken your position and cause you to be pulled off balance if the horse is at all lively.

Face the horse directly, or, if you wish to emphasize forward movement in the horse, then turn your right shoulder (if lungeing to the left) a little toward him. If, however, you are having difficulty steadying his paces then turn your left shoulder toward him (this again on the left rein). Reverse this process on the right rein if necessary.

REIN CONTACT

The aim here is much the same as in riding the horse, a steady elastic feel is sought.

THE WHIP

On the left rein the whip is held in the right hand and for the most part is pointed downward and towards the horse's hocks to indicate to him to go forward. Do not wave the whip constantly as this will have the same effect on your horse as incessant use of the leg when riding. When asking the horse to increase his pace or make a transition to a higher pace, lift the whip smoothly forward and up toward the horse. The whip should only serve to emphasise your voice commands. If of course the horse does not respond and you feel it necessary to use the whip then flick it smoothly but quickly once only. Use it together with the voice command, striking the horse immediately beneath the point of the hock. As soon as you see or feel the horse respond return the whip to its original position.

THE VOICE

Observe carefully the effect your voice has on the horse. The tone you use is most important. The words you use should always be the same as the horse will become used to the sound of them (for instance if you always say "whoa" to stop him then there is no reason to suddenly change this to "halt").

When you wish the horse to increase speed, impulsion, or make a change to a higher pace use a sharper tone. Do not raise the pitch of the voice as this is likely to make the horse nervous. If you have a naturally high pitched voice then you will need to lower it whilst dealing with your horse. When asking the horse to slow down use a long drawn out command. The moment the horse begins to respond to each command, praise him enthusiastically.

HALF HALTS

Before issuing any direct command to your horse, always proceed by preparing the horse. On the lunge this is done by the use of the word a - n - d spoken in a long drawn out manner. This will ensure the horse's attention is brought to you and not elsewhere. This verbal half-halt gives the horse a moment to collect himself both physically and mentally and prepare for what comes next.

OBJECTIVES

What then are we working towards in the regular lungeing of our horse?

IN THE EARLY STAGES

The horse learns to relate to his trainer and obey his commands with confidence and alacrity. At this stage the trainer must be a very experienced person able to control his own voice, bodily movements, and have a heightened sense of the effect his own mental and physiological state has on the horse. The horse will be worked initially without the burden of saddle, bridle or rider. He will learn self carriage in a confined area and will begin to build the muscles needed to carry these. By working the horse on his own on the lunge you will help him to develop an awareness of his own body and how to improve his balance and co-ordination.

These early lessons are, for the horse, a vital part of his training. If neglected or carried out incorrectly the horse could be harmed, both physically and mentally. It is amazing how many horses and riders have only a vague understanding of the aids and their proper effects. Years spent in confusion and disharmony could easily be avoided with the correct knowledge to start with.

LATER ON IN THE HORSE'S TRAINING

At this stage we are looking to improve his paces. Again, the more experienced the handler the quicker and more effective the results.

If you are relatively inexperienced at lungeing, try not to be put off by thinking yourself not good enough; persevere and if you do encounter difficulties, find someone to help. Who knows, maybe you too will be able to help someone else in the future!

SETTING THE HORSE IN MOTION

This can be a little tricky, especially for the inexperienced. It is no good standing and waving the whip, expecting the horse to understand. He will probably only back away from you in horror.

To set the horse off as smoothly as possible:

1. Face him straight in the direction you wish him to go. Make sure he is standing attentively and not looking the opposite way at the view. Begin on the rein you feel the horse will be the happiest on. For the majority of horses this is likely to be the left.

Check tack — Before asking the horse to move off, make sure your tack is safely and correctly fitted. Check the girth or roller for comfort and security. The cavesson should be firm with its throatlash fastened across the cheeks, keeping the cheekpiece well away from the horse's eyes. The noseband of the cavesson should be fitted in the same place as a cavesson noseband (two fingers width below the cheekbone) and should not move about. Make sure the side reins are properly fastened and of equal length.

2. We will assume you have positioned the horse ready to move off left. The lunge whip should at this moment be tucked under your right armpit, pointing down and back behind you. Hold the lunge line (already looped smoothly, not wrapped or muddled) in your left hand with about three feet of it between you and the horse. Ask the horse to walk on; use a firm voice and walk with him yourself for a few yards. As the horse begins to move off (do not step back yourself) draw the whip from under your right arm so you are holding it in your right hand. The whip should now be pointing towards the horse's hocks. Play out the line maintaining contact all the time; ask the horse for more impulsion with your voice and action (only) of the lunge whip.

Your body should now be turned a little with the right shoulder towards the horse. Aim to stand almost still, but do not feel you *have* to root yourself to the spot. If the horse loses impulsion or becomes worried then move with him. Similarly, if you walk too fast or straight towards the horse you will push him off balance into his outside shoulder. This has the same disastrous effect as does excessive use of the inside leg for riding into "corners" (see Chapter 8).

TO BRING THE HORSE TO HALT

Generally speaking the horse should come to halt on the command "halt" or "whoa". He should be facing the direction in which he has been travelling and not turn towards you. If you allow the horse to turn to face you when you ask him to stop (which he may do if he is a little nervous) make sure he does not walk to you unless asked to do so. Some horses develop a knack of suddenly turning inward from a walk or trot or even a canter. This can be very difficult to deal with, so it is better that the horse learns from the outset to "face front" at halt, in readiness to move on again.

BE CONSISTENT

As in riding the novice will have difficulty in the co-ordination of his aids. He will tend to make the same sort of mistakes with his horse on the lunge as he does from the saddle. At least on the lunge you have the horse in front of you, so are more likely to recognise your faults and perhaps work out for yourself how to deal with them.

The disadvantage for the novice is that when he begins lungeing he may become disappointed and so give up because he cannot at first see more than the horse going round and round. My advice would be: do not give up at this point but persevere; after a few sessions you should begin to make some observations.

The first thing you will notice is that the rhythm of the paces becomes more even. Also, the horse will begin to stretch forward occasionally with his head and neck. He may also champ at his bit.

STIFF SIDE, BEST SIDE

You should also now have some idea which rein the horse feels and looks best on. (See also Chapter 8). The contact you feel along the rein will help you decide this. The horse will feel heavier in the hand when his weight is carried on his outside shoulder, i.e., when lungeing to the left his weight is displaced onto the right shoulder, so he feels as if he is trying to pull away from your left hand.

N.B. The right side is the stiff side here. The same applies when you are riding. If you look carefully you will see that the rest of the horse from the girth area back will be angled towards you.

If you are lungeing on a soft surface you will be able to see that the hind hoofprints will be somewhat to the left of the front ones. To correct this lack of straightness bring the forehand further over with your left hand to bring him into line with his quarters. You may have to pull quite hard but make sure you do not either jerk or use a pull and release motion. You may have to repeat this shifting of the forehand during several lunge sessions, so do take care not to upset him, especially about the head. Do not worry if you lose the steady rhythm of the pace for a while, it is more important to supple the horse first. To improve the "stiffness" on the right rein (recognised by the horse falling towards you) again take pulls at the rein but this time with the intention of bending the neck which will encourage the muscles on the right side of the neck to be activated and those on the left to stretch. You may have to walk around a little more to achieve this but again do not worry. This exercise is best begun at a walk to give the horse a chance to understand what you are asking. You will find that once you are able to use this exercise at a trot the horse will take *himself* out onto the circle.

The worst mistake for the handler to make is to try to stand absolutely still regardless of what the horse is doing. You *are* aiming to eventually be able to stand in one place but *only* when the horse is sufficiently supple on both sides of his body and level in his paces. This will enable him to execute the true circle.

LOOKING FOR REAL IMPROVEMENT

So what are the signs that your horse is improving on the lunge? We have already discussed suppleness on each rein along each side of the horse's body; now we need to look to the topline of the horse. This will be somewhat improved by lateral suppleness.

STRAIGHT LINES

You can by means of the lunge, work the horse along straight lines. To do this you need to have the horse working well on the circle first. To put him on a straight line make sure

1. You have the space to do so. (The support of a hedge or fence or even a line of poles about a foot off the ground will be a guide).
2. You increase your own pace and raise the whip, ease the rein without dropping the contact. This should be sufficient to put him onto a straight line.
3. After fifteen metres or so return the horse to a circle by slowing your own pace. (Take care not to step back). Maintain the horse's impulsion and bring his head and neck around to the shape of the circle. Use an open rein aid by taking the rein hand out away from your body; i.e., right hand to the right, left hand to the left.

N.B. Open rein aids described in following chapter.

Repeat the above exercise until you can do so really smoothly, then try some alterations within the pace at walk and trot to begin with. These are described in Chapter 9.

SUMMARY

Remember to keep increasing impulsion by use of the driving aids. Aids should always be smooth but positive. Watch the horse constantly for his reactions to you and learn to recognise when he is puzzled by your instructions. Any roughness or signs of temper will be counter productive as the horse will think only of his fear and not of what you are trying to tell him. You should eventually be able to put the horse wherever you like within your restricted area. Once you are able to do this without either upsetting him or losing the fluency of his paces, then you are ready to lunge him over poles and caveletti. In Chapter 12 you will find ideas on the layout of athletic exercises.

LUNGEING PROBLEMS

The horse that is difficult to keep going or refuses to lunge at all:

Likely Causes

1. If you have owned your horse from the very early stages of his training you will probably be quite conversant with lungeing. If, however, you acquired the horse since he was "broken in" you may not know how much lungeing he was given, if it was done correctly or indeed at all! In this case you will have a problem, but not necessarily a big one.

   If the horse really is difficult you will need a sensible assistant to lead the horse whilst you teach him the commands you intend to use. The assistant should lead him from the outside so that the horse may focus his attention entirely on you. To this purpose alone also he or she should hold the horse only lightly on the rein or side rein and be silent. All talking should be left to you, the handler.

   Once the horse becomes conversant with the commands of whoa/halt, walk on, trot on, etc., on both reins (*do not* consider cantering until you are really proficient and the horse well balanced — not just quiet!) ask the assistant to melt quietly into the background.

2. A horse may take exception to being lunged if the handler tries to put him on too small a circle. The horse may keep pulling away from your hand or swing his quarters away in order to avoid the degree of collection being imposed upon him.

3. If the handler walks forward towards the horse too much he poses a threat; this will also cause the horse to back away.

THE HORSE WHICH IS DIFFICULT TO SLOW DOWN

A horse which rushes round and round can be most annoying, if not unnerving. If the horse is very strong also, he may pull away from you. Most important here then is to keep the horse's head towards you. If you find this a problem then take steady, extra pulls from the contact you already have. By this I do not mean, loose, tight, loose, tight. Make sure you maintain a bend in your elbow and a slight curve of the wrist so that as in riding you are able to follow and allow forward movement in the horse.

If the horse seems genuinely frightened and will not slow down, do try to be as calm as possible. Any sign of temper or even slight frustration will convey itself to the horse and only serve to delay the proceedings.

Try the following: Maintain a steady rein contact, keep an even tone of voice. The whip should be kept very low or even tucked away behind you under the armpit of the spare hand.

Remember, the position of your body can also help to slow the horse (see page 80). Never jerk at the horse's head because you are annoyed that he will not obey your commands. Slow him gradually by decreasing the size of the circle; turn your shoulder towards his head *or* guide him steadily towards the nearest hedge or fence so that the horse feels blocked and is obliged to slow down. Take care here that the horse does not think you are trying to chase him into a corner but understands that you wish him to slow down. Do not drop the rein contact or walk towards him until he stops or steadies to the speed you require. If the horse does panic and rush round then keep calm and repeat the procedure next time round.

THE HORSE WHICH IS DIFFICULT TO KEEP GOING ON THE LUNGE

To enliven a horse which dislikes being lunged can also be a difficult task. There may be several reasons for this:

1. The horse may never have been taught to lunge correctly; in this case follow the procedure as described on page 86.
2. You may be doing something which is confusing the horse. Here it is up to you to work out what it is that is causing the confusion. Maybe you walk about too much but fail to actually drive the horse forward correctly.
3. You may be asking the horse to work on too small a circle. Less than fifteen metres would certainly be detrimental to the horse's progress unless he is very supple.
4. You may have a horse which will lunge in one direction and not the other. Here again follow the advice given on page 86. Once you have succeeded in keeping the horse on the move, then try the suppling exercises on page 84.

SUMMARY

As most problems encountered are the direct result of ignorance, either blissful or otherwise, it is up to the handler to find his/her way to the root of the problem. To decide if you yourself are at fault, or if a previous owner caused the horse to become confused or even frightened.

CHAPTER 8

MOVEMENT AND
FURTHER SCHOOLING

FORWARD MOVEMENT OF THE HORSE

What is it? If you are to be successful in schooling your horse, and indeed improving yourself, then you must learn what is forward movement. Without this there can be no real improvement for horse or rider. Forward movement has little to do with actual speed, though this may be all you have initially. There is a world of difference between the horse going along when you ask him and truly going forward. The horse which does "go forward" is a joy to observe and to ride. He looks and feels powerful, athletic, buoyant yet totally controlled. Some horses possess a natural "spring" in their stride, but this can be produced in many, many more with correct training. Part of the enjoyment of schooling with your own horse lies in finding out just what he is capable of. It *is* possible to produce from a less than perfect looking animal a confident, powerful, naturally elegant horse. Do not give up easily just because you think your horse is not well bred enough!

THE HORSE NOT GOING FORWARD

In order to find out whether the horse goes forward we need to look first of all at those which do not. Consider the following examples:

1. The horse seems obedient to your aids (this applies both on the flat and whilst jumping) but in a competitive situation results seem rather disappointing. Taking into account your own nerves it is likely that this horse goes more easily at home because he is on familiar territory. It does show, however, that he is not truly going forward but working mechanically and well below his capabilities.
2. However hard you work on your horse, he never quite seems to "get going". You find that if you stop using your legs, he slows down or stops. This horse obviously does not go forward as he cannot carry himself without the support of his rider's leg.
3. Your horse may seem rather "strong" in your hands. He may when you try to apply leg aids, rush off and anticipate; when jumping, he seems only to feel comfortable if he is going at speed.
4. Goes quietly for a while, then all of a sudden starts misbehaving.

There are other problems such as these which can be overcome by positive forward riding. These include "bucking", napping, running out instead of jumping, and lack of confidence, particularly on the road.

WATCH OTHERS

Observe others and look at the overall togetherness of horse and rider. Look at the horse's hindlegs. Do they step positively well under his body? Do his hindquarters look as if they belong to his front end or does he look like two separate animals? Train yourself to look further than the head carriage of the horse. It is simple enough to persuade the horse to carry his head "in", but a very self-defeating exercise.

TO RIDE THE HORSE FORWARD

When applying your leg aids, try to decide whether the reaction of the horse is the correct one. He should "spring forward" without rushing or undue hesitation. As you gain in experience, you will feel the propulsion as the horse lowers his quarters and "pushes" off his hindlegs to go forward. This forward propulsion is then contained, maintained or allowed to "ooze" through the rider's softened rein contact, according to the horse's response to his rider's driving aids. If you feel that your horse does not respond in the right way to your leg or rein aids, make sure you are giving the correct aids. Check also your position, especially your hands. For the rider to know and feel what is true forward movement in the horse may take months, years of determined self and horse analysis. Many riders and indeed trainers never learn what it means. If they did, there would be fewer problems in the British Horse World today.

MAKING THE AIDS WORK

RIDING STRAIGHT LINES

The horse must be able to go absolutely straight. His hindlegs should follow the tracks made by his forelegs. To be able to remain straight the horse must be equally supple along each side of his body as well as along his topline (that is, from his ears along his back to his tail).

If you ride or school your horse in an open field, as a guide to riding straight look at a fence post, a tree or some point ahead of you. If riding in an arena or indoor school, ride straight lines without the support of the wall. (If, when you ask your horse to go straight he leans his weight on one shoulder and shifts his quarters the opposite

Figure 8-1 Beginnings of Forward Movement

Note:

True forward movement in the horse may be difficult to know and feel in the early stages of riding.

way, it shows a "stiffness" along the side that he is leaning toward, and is sometimes referred to as "one sided").

So, if the horse carries his weight on his left shoulder, his quarters will probably be to the right. In order to make him go consistently straight, the horse must be made more supple by making turns and circles, particularly on the stiff side, using an open rein aid. (See page 94). A temporary correction would be for the rider to use a more active left leg to push the horse's left hindleg further under his body towards his left foreleg and open the right rein and support with the left as a direct rein. The horse will probably feel heavier on your left hand as his weight is carried on this shoulder.

N.B. Make sure you do not push his quarters over the opposite way, but always align the forehand instead. Make sure also that in opening the right rein you do not bend his neck to the right, as this will only shift his quarters left.

As you open the rein, the horse's neck should become centrally placed. (Maintain a firm but not "pulling" contact). If the horse still will not become straight, then he is not "springing" off your leg aid sufficiently. Do take care, in that whatever rein aid you give, your hands do not fall below the horse's line of contact. If you are unsure where that is, ride your horse with your hands at slightly different levels and note his reactions.

ABOUT TURNS AND CIRCLES

You will see from the correct photograph overleaf that the horse should turn his head (keeping the face vertical) and bend his neck into the shape of the turn or circle. His hindlegs directly propel his forehand into that turn (so the hindfeet should follow the tracks made by the forefeet). When making a turn to the right, the muscles along the right side of his body shorten and those along the left side lengthen. The pace, whether it be walk, trot or canter should be even, rhythmical and forward going. The word "bend" is loosely used in the horse world. The horse cannot actually bend his whole body. His neck can bend and the quarters can shift, thus giving the illusion of bending.

REASONS FOR TEACHING THE HORSE
TO "BEND" CORRECTLY

If he does not move equally well in both directions, it means that he will be insufficiently pliant, supple and unlikely to "build" muscle as he should. Think of your horse as an athlete and the schooling that you do as suppling and preparatory for all kinds of work. Many problems in

Figure 8-2 Passive Riding

Note:
In this photo the rider has remained passive so the horse in 'falling in' with her weight shifted toward the left shoulder and head turned to the right.

Figure 8-3 Rider Correcting Fault

The rider is correcting the above 'wrong bend' (*Fig. 8-2*).

Figure 8-4 Correct Right Turn

Line of Bend — Novice Horse   Line of Bend — Advanced Horse

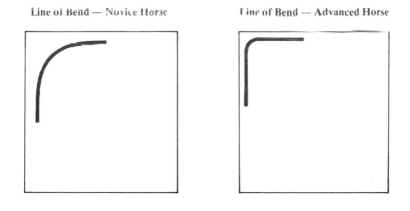

DIAGRAM 14 Line of Bend

dressage and jumping can be linked to horses being insufficiently agile and muscled *before* they begin demanding work.

INCORRECT BEND

Look now at the photographs and diagrams of a horse turning "stiffly". The horse that does not bend correctly in both directions will make a turn either by (a) leaning his weight over his inside shoulder, shortening his strides and turning his head and neck away from the turn. He will tilt his whole ribcage (the area over which his rider is sitting) over towards the turn, causing the inside foreleg to be placed under the body. This means the horse's weight is not evenly balanced on all four legs; (b) appearing to bend his neck in the direction of the turn, but in reality he tilts his head so only his chin is towards the turn. This balance is then leaning on his outside shoulder. His quarters will then be towards the inside of the turn. (He may even use this turn opposite to the direction you are asking).

RECOGNISE CORRECT TURNS FOR YOURSELF

If you are unsure whether your horse does bend correctly then begin at a walk, ride straight lines and turns on both reins. Look at the horse's head and neck and see if he really bends his whole neck. Try also to see or feel where his shoulders are as you turn. Then try this exercise at trot and canter. See, also, if you can tell what happens to his hindquarters as you turn.

AIDS FOR CORRECT TURNS

The aids that you give are those sufficient to make the horse the desired shape of the turn or circle.

Inside Leg   Activate's the horse's inside hindleg.

Inside Rein   Asks the horse to turn his head and bend his neck in the direction of the turn. This rein may be used as an open rein or direct rein aid.

Open Rein   This should be used on horses (whatever their age) which lack suppleness on turns and circles. Apply this rein aid by moving your inside hand *as far sideways* (not backwards) as will cause the horse to bend his neck. Remember to use your inside leg first before applying the rein aid.

Direct Rein   Can be used once the horse accepts easily the rider's hand

94

and will turn smoothly and correctly. Apply this aid by closing the fingers of the inside hand. If you are unsure what is the correct rein aid for your horse at the moment, then experiment by making turns and circles on both reins, using first a direct rein then an open rein. (Begin at walk). He may even need a direct rein aid on one rein but an open rein on the other, or he may vary from one pace to another.

Outside Leg The rider's outside leg is intended to control the horse's quarters, but do not worry too much if you have difficulty in keeping your leg in the correct position. Basically, the horse will swing his quarters out (say to the right), if he is stiff along his left side. Your main objective is then to make him move supple along this "stiff" side. You will find if you make constant open rein turns, he will become more supple and level, his quarters will line themselves up to his forehand.

Outside Rein Assists in allowing or correcting the amount of bend in the neck. Also this rein may assist in keeping the horse's head straight and help maintain the rhythm and balance of his paces.

HOW MUCH BEND?

The horse at the beginning of his training or re-training learns to work slight curves whilst the horse who has progressed to an advanced state will be able to shorten through his body to a greater degree. (See Diagram 14).

A FEW WORDS OF CAUTION

The horse should never be pushed out into the corners of your arena in an effort to force the correct shape. This will only result in the horse over-shortening his stride and developing long-term tensions throughout his body which will inhibit his progress. For dressage, you will experience difficulties later in the horse's training in achieving alterations in the horse's balance, in the lengthening and shortening of his stride and progress to two-track work. Also, do not use markers to ride around the outside of as the horse will tense and swing away from them. If jumping is to be the horse's job in life, then early tensions as described will limit his athletic ability and scope.

RIDING THE TURN OR CIRCLE

Before actually turning make sure you create plenty of impulsion (you may only get speed to start with but if you keep asking, the horse will realise what you want by the constant repetition of your aids) then make a half halt (see Chapter 4), apply the leg and reins as described, remembering that the leg aids must precede the rein aids. Make sure the horse leads into the bend by turning his head (keeping it vertical) and bending the whole of his neck (see Figs. 8-2 & 8-3). If the horse still has difficulty bending his neck, then open the inside rein (make sure you do not straighten the wrist or pull downwards) and push his neck round by sliding your outside hand slowly but firmly from withers almost to his poll. Return the hand *smoothly* back to contact. Repeat this at regular intervals until the horse understands what you are asking. You may find when you begin the early suppling work that the circles end up smaller than you intend. Do not worry about this but make sure you do not pull the horse sharply round. If you are working in trot or canter and having difficulty making a correct "bend" then keep returning to walk and showing the horse again what it is you require. Make sure you do not pull or push the horse first outwards then inward before the turn. All you will do is to unbalance his weight from one shoulder to the other which will cause him to shorten his stride and lose all forward impetus. You could try riding a threepenny bit (hexagonal) shape: make a bend where the points are, then a straight line, then a bend, and so on. This will help ensure you do not push the horse outwards before each turn. Do not worry if the horse rushes to begin with; this means only that he is experiencing difficulty in using his tense muscles. Also, do not worry about controlling his quarters over much in the initial stages. You will find that as long as you bend his neck and continually ask him to go forward, he will bring his quarters into line with his forehand of his own accord.

The rider's aim towards the end of the basic training is to execute a true circle. That is one in which the horse's hindlegs remain directly in track with his forelegs. The riding of a hexagonal shape as described is excellent as it puts less strain on the hind limbs.

As the horse's muscles develop and strengthen you will find he is able to remain in a steady rhythm and outline throughout a circle.

SIZE OF CIRCLES

The curves at first cover an overall area of twenty metres (or even more if you have an excitable horse).

The circles can gradually be reduced until during the latter stages he is able to describe a small circle (described as a volte) of eight to ten metres. On no account should you try to make the horse work on small circles until he remains constant in outline as well as active and supple on larger ones.

EXERCISES TO HELP YOU ASSESS THE HORSE'S ABILITY TO EXECUTE A "TRUE" CIRCLE

ALSO TO IMPROVE ACTIVITY AND SO ENGAGE THE HINDLEGS

1. Begin at walk, then trot making hexagonal shapes. Do these on both reins. Check impulsion by pushing the horse on a little, then reduce the pace by using half halts.
2. As the horse becomes constant during the above take him from a twenty metre circle to a fifteen metre one and back to twenty metres again. Complete two twenty-metre circles to one fifteen-metre circle.

N.B. Maintain the bend to the degree the horse feels capable of throughout the exercise. This exercise can be used later in the training, from fifteen metres to ten metres and vice versa. When you think the horse is able, try the above exercise in canter.

CHAPTER 9

THE PACES

PACES

It is not possible to learn to ride entirely from books, as there is no substitute for practical experience. The rider can, however, go a long way to help himself by trying to create a visual "picture" in his mind by whatever means available to him. This may be partly from reading books and magazine articles and having riding instruction on his own or other horses of varying standards. He may learn also by observing others. Whilst discussing the horse's paces, I shall give some indications to help the rider discover for himself how good his horse's paces are and how to improve them.

ABOUT THE WALK

Is a pace of four time; this means there are four distinct hoof beats. These are left hind, left fore, right hind, right fore. You can see from the diagram (below) that although each leg moves separately, it is a hindleg which propels the foreleg forward on the same side. Though it is easier for the rider to work on his own position at the walk, it is more difficult for him to assess his horse at this pace. The rider is aiming that the horse should move with even, elastic steps maintaining an even rhythm and steady head and neck.

Footfalls at Walk

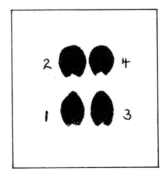

DIAGRAM 15

TO HELP THE RIDER ASSESS THE QUALITY OF THE WALK:
Experiment with the Following Exercises

A *Ask the horse to walk on faster and more impulsively than normal (do not allow the reins to loosen). If the horse resists, or breaks into trot, use the back bracing aids followed immediately by more leg.*

B *Now try walking slower than normal (maintain impulsion in the walk). Here the horse should take a stronger contact so take care not to 'drop' him or you will also lose the impulsion.*

1. Try riding the above exercises (**A** & **B**) first with hands higher than usual, then lower.
2. Try **A** & **B** with your hands wider apart, then closer together.
3. Try making the rein contact tighter.
4. Try a rein contact that is softer than you usually use.
5. When on a turn or circle, try also an open rein and a direct rein. Alter how much or little leg you use throughout the above exercises. Ride the exercises on straight lines, turns and circles and give yourself and your horse time to learn something from each. This means you obviously do not do them all in the same riding session or you will only confuse yourself and your horse. Give the horse time to adjust to the alterations and try them also in trot and in canter. These alterations within the pace teach the horse to propel himself forward from his hindlegs and also to shift his balance back. They will increase the length of the horse's stride and teach him the use of all his muscles. They will give the rider a visual guide to assist him towards feeling what is good and what is not so good.

THE HORSE'S REACTIONS TO YOU

Try to decide when you ride the horse in any way different from usual, whether *his* resulting reactions are because:
1. The exercise will be useful, but the horse's initial reaction is that he finds what you are asking is rather difficult.
2. The exercise really is too difficult for the horse at the moment; so leave it for a few weeks then try asking again.
3. The exercise may be used but to a lesser or greater degree.
4. The exercise is really helpful therefore may be made use of during the schooling of your horse.

SUMMARY

Do allow at least two minutes on each rein for each part of the above exercises. Again do not use them all in one schooling session or you may find the horse (and you) will become confused.

THE WALK ON A LONG REIN

The rider closes the lower leg and allows the reins to ease through his fingers. Allow the horse to stretch his neck until his nose is about level with his knees. The walk should be forward going but remain in a steady rhythm. Use this walk during your usual schooling routine. If the horse does not stretch as you lengthen the rein, then either (a) he is not using the muscles along his topline (ears to tail) and therefore is too "tight" and unable to stretch, or (b) you may have used too little or too much leg through the transition from the walk to the walk on a long rein, or (c) you may have released the rein too quickly and lost impulsion and contact with the horse's mouth. When included in a dressage test, the walk on a long rein indicates to the judge that the elasticity in the horse's muscles allow them to stretch and shorten smoothly when asked, without the horse losing his balance and increasing speed.

Figure 9-1 Long rein walk. Horse stretches but remains "on contact".

100

THE WALK ON A LOOSE REIN

The rider holds the reins at the buckle and allows the horse to lower his head and stretch his neck well down. This allows the horse to relax after a period of work of a more collected nature.

N.B. Do not ride along the road with loose reins even if you think the road is quiet and the horse under control. A sudden distraction, however slight, may cause the horse to slip or stumble. (Though the reins are not and indeed cannot stop the horse from slipping, they will help him to maintain his co-ordination, concentration and balance).

(Courtesy Colne Valley Riding Stables)

Figure 9-2 Loose Rein Walk

Note:

Rein contact given away; horse allowed to relax between short work sessions and at end of schooling.

N.B. Not advised on the road. Note maintained forward movement and activity of hindlimbs.

THE TROT

The trot is a pace of "two time", the horse moving his legs in diagonal pairs. The left fore and right hind make up the left diagonal, so the right diagonal is the right fore and left hind leg together. The trot is the most useful pace at which to work both horse and rider so it is well to learn as much as you can about it.

RISING TROT

The rider, with his shoulders inclined slightly forward, allows the movement of the trot to help him rise and sit smoothly. You should be aware of absorbing the spring of the movement down and forward through hip and thigh. The rider should not bump on his horse's back but be sensitive to the effect his balance and weight have on the horse. Make frequent checks on your position and the aids you are using.

RIDING ON A NAMED DIAGONAL

In order to improve your "feel" on the horse and be able to school him you need to know which pair of the horse's legs is on the ground at any given moment. During the rising trot, you will be sitting in the saddle as one pair of legs are on the ground and rising as the other pair come to the ground. This means that as you sit you influence with your seat and leg aids, one pair of legs. As you rise out of the saddle the effect of your aids is reduced. If, over a period of time, you tend to sit on the same diagonal without realising, the horse is likely to work less efficiently with one pair of his legs. This may not seem too important, but will lead to the horse working unlevel in his strides and even lead to him becoming one-sided. (See Chapter 8).

TO FIND OUT WHICH DIAGONAL
YOU ARE SITTING ON

Set off at a steady rising trot, making sure you rise evenly and do not miss a beat. To discover which diagonal you are on, look down at each of the horse's shoulders in turn. The shoulder and foreleg move back toward you as you sit. If you are on the left diagonal, then it will be the left shoulder and foreleg. When schooling your horse make a change of diagonal when you change the rein, work the horse equally in both directions. Out hacking, make frequent changes of diagonal. When schooling on the left rein, you should be sitting on the right diagonal and vice versa on the right. The purpose of using this outside diagonal is to increase the efficiency of the horse's inside hind leg which assists in correct bends and turns.

TO CHANGE DIAGONAL

During the rising trot instead of rising up and down, up down, go: up, down down up, so you miss a beat and change on to the horse's other pair of legs. You will find that for quite some time you need to remind yourself to look down and check that you are using the correct diagonal. You will also find you will eventually feel which diagonal you are on and have no need to look down. This is obviously a step towards feeling what is going on underneath you, which is after all what good riding is all about.

SITTING TROT

A difficult pace for the novice rider who is as yet unable to absorb the movement of his horse. Once you find you are able to sit down into the saddle without bumping about and upsetting the horse in any way, you can achieve a great deal more in the schooling of your horse. When you begin schooling in sitting trot, do so only for about ten minutes at a time, remembering that the horse may also be unused to this. Once correct the sitting trot enables the rider to apply his aids, particularly the leg and seat aids, with greater precision and control. He is closer to his horse, therefore able to develop greater feel.

N.B. The Chapter "Riding Without Stirrups" also gives advice when to and when not to "sit" to the trot. Also see "motion of the pelvis" — (Chapter 2).

SCHOOLING YOUR HORSE AT A TROT

Experiment with the exercises suggested in the previous paragraphs (walk). Particularly make alterations within the trot pace; see if you can make three alterations in sitting trot, as follows:

1. Begin at a trot which seems too slow. Maintain your rein contact and feel that the horse is listening to your driving aids.
2. Increase the pace, allowing a little more speed; use active but not too strong aids. Soften the rein contact only slightly as the emphasis must be on the horse's propulsion from behind.
3. Increase the pace until you are going quite fast. Maintain the contact to help the horse keep his balance. Keep the trot going until you feel a "lift" in the shoulders of the horse. Remember the back bracing aid to bring the horse back to the speed you require.

AIDS

Do not worry about riding too fast, just make sure you do not do so on a slippery or hard surface. Also make frequent checks on your aids. Try using alternate legs when asking the horse to increase. You are aiming to use your legs in time with the forward lift of each hindleg. If you cannot feel which of the hindlegs are moving at any given moment, then glance down at the horse's shoulders. Bearing in mind that the trot is a diagonal movement, use your right leg as you see the horse's left shoulder move forward. Use your left leg as you see the right shoulder move.

Try also riding through the alterations with hands fairly wide apart. (Six inches or more each side of the horse's neck). This enables you to give the horse maximum freedom of the shoulders without either loosening the contact or fear of pulling back on his mouth. The freedom of the horse's shoulders is particularly important during the early stages of the horse's training. He must learn to work the whole of his body freely without loss of balance or undue restriction. Remember the back bracing aid, use it frequently, particularly before and after each of the changes within the pace. Make sure you do not tip forward as this will inhibit the forward propulsion of the pace. Make sure you are following the trot movement by being mobile through the pelvis. When you have worked the horse on both reins and feel you have actually made positive alterations in his pace, come back to the middle pace. This is called the working trot. It should now feel more active and free going. During this resulting trot, the horse should look longer and more rounded in his neck. Make sure you sit up straight, and have the feeling there is "more horse" in front of you. If he stretches his neck and "tugs" at the bit, it shows he is using himself. Follow the movement with your hands, but make sure you do not loosen the reins. If his head seems too low, then push it up by using your legs. Do not pull the horse's head up or you will lose the forward movement you have worked so hard to achieve. You will eventually find that when you push the horse on, he will lengthen his stride without unduly increasing the speed of the pace.

SUMMARY — PURPOSE OF ALTERATIONS WITHIN A PACE

The horse should learn from the beginning of his training to propel himself forward from his hindlegs. He should also be shown how to bring his balance back again. These alterations of pace will help towards this aim. Riders who compete or hope to compete in dressage, jumping and showing competitions should find the exercises helpful, as for all these, the horse must be able to lengthen and shorten his stride and alter balance. The rider, by experimenting a little, will find schooling of greater interest as he will begin to realise many things for himself.

RHYTHM OF THE TROT

Having experimented with the above exercises, you should now be more aware of how the horse moves beneath you. Each horse has its own rhythm. The horse who has a shorter stride may appear to hurry when asked for more impulsion. Do not worry about this unduly. Keep asking the horse to push himself onto a longer stride but use half halts each time he "scuttles" too fast. The horse with a longer stride will have a slightly faster rhythm. He must not be held back but allowed to work through the full stride. (Try to find the correct working rhythm by using the above exercise for your horse, as it is from this you will be able to make real improvements in the horse's shape and way of going).

TO ASSESS THE QUALITY OF THE TROT

1. Make transitions to walk — these should be smooth, the horse maintaining a forward going even pace. He should not "lean" and fall into the walk. He should not raise his head and shorten his neck unduly, though he may do during the first few days or weeks.
2. Make transitions into canter — if the trot is good you will get smooth immediate transitions. The horse should not throw his head up and rush nor should he be reluctant to canter. If the transitions to and/or from the trot are not too good, then more work is needed on the trot.

ABOUT THE CANTER

The horse in canter propels himself forward in a series of low jumping strides. The canter is a pace of "three time". This means that each canter stride is made up of three distinct beats. The canter, as do all the paces, begins with a hindleg. If you are riding to the left, which means you require a left canter, the order or sequence of legs is as follows:

1. Outside (right) hindleg.
2. Outside diagonal (right foreleg and left hindleg together).
3. Inside foreleg (left fore).

The inside foreleg, described as the leading leg as it appears to "lead" the canter, is the last leg in each canter stride to reach the ground. There then follows a moment of suspension, when all four legs are off the ground before the sequence begins again. Reverse the sequence for a right canter.

PREPARE TO CANTER

The ability of the horse to make a smooth immediate transition to canter from halt, walk or trot depends upon his state of training and the rider's ability to "prepare" him. The pace before the canter should be active but unhurried. You should feel as if you have the horse "together" between leg and hand. If when asked to canter, the horse just increases the speed, then bring him back, increase the amount of impulsion, maintain a good rein contact and ask again. The horse should become able to make smooth transitions from walk and trot. To canter from halt, he must be *happy* to halt squarely and respond straight away from the leg and seat aids without throwing his head and heaving his forehand up. Instead the quarters lower to propel the horse.

AIDS TO CANTER

To ask your horse to canter left, cease rising, apply your left leg (inside leg) on the girth and your right leg (outside leg) behind the girth. The inside leg creates and maintains impulsion and your outside leg tells the horse to begin his canter with his outside hindleg. Your inside rein asks the horse to flex or bend in the direction of the canter (in this case, left) and your outside rein helps control the amount of bend and maintain rhythm. As the positioning of these aids are the same as for correct bend (see Chapter 8) it follows that it is the way they are applied that is important.

TO CANTER

Having asked for more impulsion, (see Chapter 8 — forward movement of the horse) from the horse, apply a half-halt (see Chapter 4) then give the canter aids.

EVEN MORE ABOUT LEG AIDS

You may either (a) use your inside leg actively and your outside leg gives a single touch or (b) having created the impulsion with the inside leg already, hold the impulsion with it and use the outside leg actively instead. The inside rein aid may be an open rein or a direct rein, as previously described, (Chapter 4, Rein Aids). The use of the open rein through the canter transition and during the canter will allow the horse freedom of the inside (leading) shoulder and foreleg, providing the rider maintains steady contact. This may make a deal of difference to the fluency of the canter, particularly on a circle. The outside rein helps maintain the horse's balance and impulsion. If the rider loosens either

Figure 9-3 The Horse in Left Canter

Figure 9-4 The Horse in Right Canter

107

rein whilst asking for the canter, the horse is likely to tip forward and increase speed, rather than bend his hindlegs, lower his quarters, and push himself into canter.

N.B. The experienced rider will be able to "feel" when the horse's outside hindleg is about to step under his body and so give the aids, as in (a). The less experienced rider may find the aids as described in (b) more useful until he is able to "feel" more of what the horse's legs, particularly the hindlegs, are doing.

LEADING LEG

You may be able to feel whether your horse is on the correct leg. If not, look down (without tipping your body forward) at the inside shoulder and foreleg, which will move forward, appearing to "lead" the way.

THE RIDER'S POSITION THROUGHOUT THE TRANSITION AND DURING THE CANTER

Make sure you do not tip forward and loosen the rein contact or the horse will drop onto his forehand and feel unable to canter without increasing speed. The rider's upper body should remain upright, keep your shoulders and hips as level as possible, make frequent mental checks on the whole of your position and the aids you are giving. Try to concentrate on following the movement through the movement of hip and pelvis.

CANTER PROBLEMS

The canter for many riders is a difficult pace to establish and maintain. Here are a few problems and some ideas to help you cope with them.

HORSE WHICH IS DIFFICULT TO MAKE CANTER

If your horse will not canter when you ask him, then he is not responding correctly to your aids. He may be confused by:
1. Rider's aids which are not positive enough; or
2. Aids which are conflicting, that is you may be pulling the reins (particularly pulling backwards on the inside rein) whilst giving leg and seat aids.
3. Being too much on his forehand, therefore when he is asked to canter, he increases speed and ends up even more on his forehand, with his hindquarters trailing behind.

To Improve the Above

Consider the way in which you use your leg aids. If you are constantly pushing whilst in walk and trot, the horse will become less and less responsive. Lighten the use of leg and if the horse does not listen, support this lighter leg aid with a sharp short rap with a Schooling Whip used *close to* and simultaneously with the leg. *Maintain a firm rein contact throughout this.* Do transitions from walk to trot and trot to walk. Once the horse becomes more responsive, then ask again for the canter. This may take minutes, hours or days according to the proficiency and determination of the rider.

CANTERING ON THE "WRONG" LEG

The horse, when asked to canter, say to the left, persists in cantering with his right fore leading. As it is the horse's right hindleg which begins the left canter, it follows that this hindleg was not positioned in the correct place when the canter aid was given. This may be caused by the rider pulling back or down with the inside hand which "blocks" the freedom of forward movement in the horse's inside shoulder and foreleg. He will swing his quarters away, which means that instead of his outside hindleg being under your outside leg aid, his inside hind will be there instead. You will get a wrong sequence of legs and so a wrong canter. Lack of suppleness in the horse may cause him to canter on the wrong leg. Improve the impulsion and correct bend in trot. Work particularly on the horse's "stiff" side (the side toward which he "leans" the most). Be constantly reminding and correcting your own position and co-ordination of aids.

As a temporary correction for the horse who persistently canters on the wrong leg, try the following:

1. Keep the neck and head turned towards the leg you wish the horse to canter on but hold the outside rein tighter and take it out slightly. By doing this, you are aligning the horse's forehand to his quarters. Now give the canter leg aids; or

2. Stay in a rising trot throughout preparation and the transition to canter. Ride on the *inside* diagonal. You are then influencing more the outside hindleg, which is the one you wish to begin the canter; or

3. Place a pole on the ground on a curve, approach at a "strong" trot, ask for canter as you go over the pole. The horse should take a small "jump" over the pole and land with the correct leg leading. Remember to praise the horse (use your voice so you can concentrate and not lose the canter) instantly he strikes off correctly.

DIFFICULTY MAINTAINING CANTER

If the horse keeps falling into trot instead of remaining in canter until he is asked to trot, try riding with a more firm rein contact and supporting your leg aids with a long Schooling Whip. Keep your shoulders back and sit well down. If you still have problems then do more work at walk and trot, practise the variations of pace, as described previously.

HORSE WHICH RUSHES INTO CANTER
AND CANTERS TOO FAST

There are a variety of reasons why the horse does this. Consider:
1. *If his balance is on his forehand*, he will not be able to maintain a steady pace, as the hindlegs are out behind. He will be taking "short", "choppy" strides which push the quarters up. The horse will push himself onto his forehand.
2. *If he is lacking suppleness*, and sufficient muscle, he will canter in a rather stilted short striding manner. He may toss his head up and down or pull at his rider's hand. He will "lean" towards the direction of the canter. Whilst you are in canter, keep both legs close to the horse, do not take them completely away, but do not push if the horse runs from the leg. Make frequent back bracing aids. Maintain a steady rein contact; on no account pull back as this will cause the horse to tense even more. Ride straight lines and turns or a threepenny bit (hexagonal) shape to improve any suppleness. Stay in canter for as long as it takes (it may take half an hour!) to show signs of settling. Work equally on both reins. A word of caution here: do not be misled into thinking that when the horse goes quietly, he is going well. You have succeeded when you can apply your leg and seat or hand aids without him "fizzing" again.

Other problems connected to the canter, such as bucking, napping sideways, disunited canter (when the horse changes legs in front or behind making the canter suddenly feel odd) will also be helped by *positive* work at walk and trot. Make alterations through walk and trot as described previously. So if you have any particular problems connected with the canter, work at walk and trot and *leave* the canter schooling for a week or two or even longer if necessary.

110

QUARTERS IN, IN CANTER

The horse carries his quarters in advance of his forehand. This is a common fault often caused by the rider trying to make the horse canter in a more collected nature than he is ready for. The horse has to compensate for being unable to carry his quarters under his body by shifting them to one side or the other. This is usually the inside, which enables him to keep balance with his "leading" leg.

TO STRAIGHTEN THE CANTER

A temporary correction would be to tighten the outside rein contact and move your inside rein to open rein position, which moves the forehand into line with the quarters. In the long term the horse's way of going should be improved by encouraging him to work in a longer outline. Do this by making alterations in the canter pace, as follows.

Once in canter, push the horse on to a faster canter with a longer rein if he will take it (this may not be immediately); when you wish to turn, keep the legs firmly on and brace your back to bring the horse to a slower canter. Once on the straight, push the horse on again. Repeat this "going on" and slowing down exercise several times. If the horse starts to anticipate the increase of pace and becomes over excited, make less difference in the paces and more turns. Try to remain in canter if you can until the horse settles and will attempt the exercise sensibly.

N.B. If you are unsure whether the canter is improving and becoming more straight, then have someone watch you throughout this exercise.

CHAPTER 10

TRANSITIONS

A transition is a change from one pace to another or a change within a pace. The changes may be progressive or non-progressive.

PROGRESSIVE TRANSITIONS UP

A progressive transition is one that follows on logically and naturally on to a higher pace. These are halt to walk-on, walk to trot, trot to canter, canter to gallop.

PROGRESSIVE TRANSITIONS DOWN

Reverse above.

NON-PROGRESSIVE TRANSITIONS

These are changes from one pace to another, omitting one or two paces between, for instance, halt to trot, trot to halt, walk to canter, canter to walk, halt to canter, canter to halt.

WHERE POSITIVE ALTERATIONS WITHIN THE
PACE ARE REQUIRED

In dressage there are four recognised walks: collected, medium, extended and free walk. The trots are collected, working, medium and extended. The canters are collected, working, medium and extended.

Obviously, during the early training of your horse, you are not expecting to obtain all these paces. You can, however, make two, three or even four alterations of pace during walk, trot and canter. This will help you towards a greater feel and awareness of what your horse is capable of, and so enable you to work toward the correct paces. It will assist the horse to work with greater concentration and attentiveness to his rider, therefore making him more alert and obedient. Alterations within the pace will teach the horse to propel from behind as you ask him to increase and to shift himself back towards his quarters as you bring him to the slower paces.

Make the alterations on straight lines and, where possible, on curves. Alterations are discussed in the previous chapter dealing with the horse's paces.

RIDING TRANSITIONS

The most important part of any transition is the rider's ability to *prepare* his horse.

Halt to Walk-on

Check your position, rein contact and feel you have your horse's attention. Push the knee down the saddle and close the legs. If the horse does not respond and walk-on immediately, either (a) the halt was not square, therefore he had to lift his hindlegs under his body *before* he could move off; or (b) he was not paying attention, therefore was unaware of your aids; (c) your aids were not clear; (d) he is unsure of the aids, therefore you need to repeat them or support them by using your voice and/or schooling whip.

Figure 10-1 The Horse Well Placed in Halt and Ready to Walk On

113

Walk to Trot

Prepare the horse, make sure you have his attention, check your position, aids and contact. Make sure you have impulsion but not too much speed in the walk before you ask him to trot.

Trot to Canter

As in the previous transition, but the trot to canter may be more difficult for the following reasons:
1. The novice rider may have difficulty co-ordinating his aids. He should therefore practise his work at a trot and the walk to trot, trot to walk transitions and improve them first.
2. The young horse may lose his balance and increase his speed, particularly if he has a novice rider. (See Chapter 9 about the canter).
3. The horse who is stiff and tense may also "run" into canter or throw his head up above his bit and, therefore, make a rough transition. This horse will need more work on his walk and trot, paying particular attention to making him more supple and able to "bend" in both directions.

Canter to Gallop

Many people think that the horse can gallop on quite easily. In truth, the horse in his natural state will probably only gallop in fear. Anyone who has ever been on a horse which gallops off without warning, will know the feeling of uncontrolled power this evokes. The domesticised horse of today's world of ever-diminishing space, inhibited by fence and ditch, has to be taught to gallop yet stay balanced. The rider needs to be able to alter the speed and impulsion within the canter pace so that the horse learns gradually to build up speed but will "come back" to his rider when asked.

N.B. Do not gallop or ask your horse to gallop unless you know he is fairly fit. You will only do internal and external damage which may not seem immediately apparent.

When you begin to teach the horse to gallop, only ask for a few hundred yards at first. Make sure you have a "strong" impulsive canter with the horse feeling light and responsive to your leg and seat. Allow the horse to lean on your hand, do not drop him with your hand as you will encourage him to lose balance and even fall. Sit well down *but not heavily,* use active leg aids (you may need the support of your whip *tactfully* to exaggerate to the horse what is required).

Gallop to Canter

Maintain support with your hand and leg and use half-halts to gradually bring him back to the canter. Do not try to pull the horse back abruptly as you are likely to put undue strain on the horse's limbs and back.

Canter to Trot

This transition is usually the most difficult to perfect. Basically the better the actual canter, the smoother the transition down. To improve the transition down, make frequent half-halts in the canter before asking for the actual transition. Make sure you do not tip forward yourself or pull back at the horse's mouth. Either way you will unbalance him.

Trot to Walk

As canter to trot.

Walk to Halt

As above.

A young or unbalanced horse may at first take a little time about his transitions. Use your common sense about how much you insist of him.

ASSESS THE QUALITY OF THE TRANSITIONS

The experienced rider is able to feel how good or bad a transition is likely to be. He can either increase the amount of impulsion or alter his horse's balance in order to improve the horse's way of going before making the actual transition.

The rider who is as yet unable to feel what is correct should watch his horse's neck and head. If the horse raises his head and hollows his neck, then the horse has overbalanced and dropped his weight onto his shoulders. This means his hindquarters are behind the horse instead of under him holding his weight and balance.

The horse may also lean quite heavily on your hand, particularly during downward transitions. Do not worry unduly about this as he will become lighter as his balance improves.

TO IMPROVE TRANSITIONS

Changes from one pace to another will be improved by (a) alterations within each pace; (b) improving the actual paces and (c) frequent half-halts to prepare the horse before making any transition.

SUMMARY

When asking a young or unbalanced horse for a transition, particularly a downward one, you will probably find that initially the whole transition, that is from the preparation to the establishing of the next pace, may take up to twenty yards. As the horse's actual paces improve, so does his balance, therefore the transitions become more immediate and smooth, until eventually they can be made at any given point.

CHAPTER 11

RIDING ON THE ROAD

Riding on the roads of today can be, even for the most competent of riders, a nervewracking experience. Most of us have, at some time, to
In this chapter we shall be concerned with some **do's** and **don't's** when hacking on the road. I shall also give advice on how to avert or control problematical situations as they occur.

DO

1. Know the rules of the road. Read the highway code and also the pamphlet available from the British Horse Society.
2. *Always* wear a *correctly* fitted hard hat or, better still, a skull cap and chin strap. Even the most sensible of horses can be taken by surprise. So do not risk injury for the sake of your own vanity!
3. Keep your horse regularly and well shod. Overlong feet will cause the horse to slip or trip. If you ride often on the road, have your blacksmith fit road studs in your horse's shoes to help prevent slipping.
4. Introduce a young horse to the sights and sounds of the roads by taking him out with a *sensible* horse as companion first.
5. *Thank* other road users who slow down or make way for you to pass in safety. There are still too many ignorant road users, car drivers and riders number among the "baddies" who have little regard for others. So a courteous wave of a hand or smile of thanks will go some way towards improving the relationship among road users.

DO NOT

1. Take a fresh horse straight out on a busy road. Ride him at home first or lunge him.
2. Take any horse out on the road if you are unsure of his obedience to your aids. Work on him at home first until he improves.
3. Ride at speed on any road. Many accidents have happened this way. Even a walk that is too hurried may cause trouble. At the very least, the hard concrete and tarmac surfaces cause undue concussion to the horse's feet and limbs.

4. Do not ride your horse in the dark unless *absolutely* necessary. If you do feel you have to, then wear reflective clothing and clearly displayed stirrup lights.
5. Do not go out on the road if you feel nervous. Ride at home until you become more confident.

THE HORSE'S BEHAVIOUR ON THE ROAD

Some horses seem to behave perfectly well at home but as soon as you take them out they become silly or nervous or even "nappy". Let us now look at these situations.

SHYING

This is a common problem and can occur for several reasons. A young horse may be genuinely nervous to all the new sights and sounds. It may be some time before he is able to cope with concentrating on his rider *and* registering all that he sees about him. His nervousness may increase if his rider becomes impatient with him or even hits him. The horse will relate being punished to the objects of his nervousness. As an example, if the horse's attention is momentarily diverted away from his rider when he sees a paper bag flapping in the hedge, the object worries him so he shys away. He then receives a smack and so becomes more nervous. The result of this is he associates flapping objects with fear and pain and so thinks they must be bad.

LACK OF CONFIDENCE

This most often shows itself on the road or in the jumping arena. So how do you know if your horse is in need of more confidence? Well, you could take a longer look at your methods of handling and riding your horse.

IN THE FIELD OR STABLE

When grooming or saddling your horse, are your movements sudden and a little rough? Watch your horse's changing expressions and his reactions to your voice, body movements and the touch of your hands. Alternatively, are the movements you make slow and hesitant? Again, observe his reactions.

Consider also whether you are consistent with your actions and the order in which you do things. The horse can become worried and even upset by the smallest change in his routine.

LUNGEING AND RIDING

Do you ride in what you consider a relaxed manner? Are your reins a little loose in the hope that the horse will in turn "relax". Try thinking of yourself driving a car or riding a bicycle. What happens if you relax? Your attention is averted and before you know it, you may find yourself in a panic situation requiring a split second decision. The rider on the road should strive, in the interests of safety of himself, his horse and other road users, to be at all times alert. He should try to develop a way of riding in which he is neither too tense nor very relaxed. Either of these extremes is likely to unnerve his horse.

SPINNING ROUND IN FRONT OF VEHICLES

This is very frightening, particularly if the horse makes a habit of it. Occasionally, you may be able to "hide" in a gateway or gap in the hedge and so avoid some situations. There will come a time though when you are unable to avoid meeting a vehicle "face to face".

SEVERE NAPPING

The horse may reach a certain point then flatly refuse to go any further for no apparent reason. Here you need to decide whether the horse is actually frightened or just being naughty. It is a help if you know when this first began so you can ascertain the cause. If you have bought a horse or pony who previously was only ridden out with others, you will need to treat him as a youngster. He will probably have been unaware of the many things to see and hear when in the company of his friends. Now, with only his new rider for support he may worry and feel unable to cope.

TO RIDE SENSIBLY ON THE ROAD

Generally speaking, if your horse feels really confident in the way you ride him at home, he should give you little cause for concern when out hacking.
1. The horse should be kept "going forward" at all times (see Chapter 8). He should be alert to your leg, seat and back aids.
2. The horse should receive confidence from a *supportive* and *constant* rein contact. To ride on a slack rein or with one rein shorter is potentially disastrous. Also, to continually pull the horse's head to the side of the road is a likely contributor to shying and napping. This will also lead to the nose becoming one-sided. (See Chapter 8).

119

3. If you carry a whip to support your leg aids, make sure it is long enough to reach down behind your calf *without* any alteration of rein contact. Try to make sure you only use the whip for the right reasons.
4. Make sure you ride on the level surface and not on the sloping camber, which is uncomfortable for the horse.
5. If you are on a busy road you cannot afford for the horse to move even a yard further out into the road so how do you cope, when he is about to shy or "nap"?

Your main objective is to make and keep the horse as straight as possible. You must use both legs, keep your weight level on both seat bones and keep his head and neck straight. Use your voice firmly but calmly. Do not raise the pitch or shout. You will find this helps you to keep calm also, as by talking you will breathe more evenly. When the horse hesitates, it is important that you do not drop the reins.

Do not pull the horse towards any object that he is shying away from. Either allow him to stand still (if he will) and then if he wants to move closer, let him. However, if there is traffic about, ride *straight* past, as described above.

N.B. Some horses cope more easily by being kept in trot. Others are best in walk. It is up to the rider to work out what is best for his particular horse.

Anticipate. Always be thinking and looking ahead. Get to know the blind corners and difficult places for your particular horse. If there are vehicles or other animals about when he is agitated, the situation becomes distinctly worsened. Remember always your own safety and that of other humans comes first (even before that of your beloved horse!) Know where you can use large gateways or gaps to escape into if necessary. Ploughed fields are also useful for a fresh or frightened horse to sober up in.

SOME ADDITIONAL ADVICE

Obviously, prevention is better than cure and, in this case, less harrowing. Here are some pointers which will ease the process of introducing a young or a nervous horse to the roads of today.

1. Ride with a Companion

To ride out with a sensible horse is the best way to start. Ride first of all with the companion on your outside to shield your horse. When he is calm (after several outings), take him slightly ahead for a while, then behind. He has a chance then to become used to seeing traffic and new sights and sounds for himself. Eventually you will be able to ride on the outside; once he is happy about this you are ready to go it alone. Make sure you only go for short hacks to start with (half-hour or so) as the concussion of the hard roads will tell on his legs. He should, however, enjoy the mental stimulus of all there is to see. If you wish to ride on grass verges to save your horse's legs, watch out for drainage gaps. Also if the grass is long, you may not be able to see if there is anything which may injure your horse's legs or feet.

2.   Get Him Used to Noise

It may help to turn the horse out in a field close to a busy road (with strong fencing of course) where he may see and hear a variety of traffic passing throughout the day. If you have permission to ride on any local farms, you can accustom the horse to tractors and other machinery. Also cows, sheep and pigs, which can cause problems when encountered unexpectedly.

CHAPTER 12

BEGIN JUMPING

JUMPING SEAT

As with everything you learn, you need a base or set of rules from which to begin. Jumping is no exception. Later, as you gain in knowledge and experience, you will develop your own style and ideas. Those who are regular spectators of show jumping competitions may have observed that each rider has his own individual style of riding, though most will have begun their careers by learning the basics first. The base from which we begin is the general purpose seat, (as described in Chapter 2) adapted to jumping by closing up the angles of our hip, knee and ankle joints in such a way as to enable us to ride our horse over a series or course of obstacles and still remain in balance and harmony with him.

This is called the **jumping seat**. It is advisable for all novice riders or those experiencing jumping problems with their horses, to adopt this position.

The jumping seat will make you more supple and secure and also strengthen your riding. Those who are new to riding in this position may find it a little strange at first, but do persevere as it is well worth it.

HOW TO PUT YOURSELF IN A JUMPING SEAT

First look at the photographs in Figures 12-2 and 12-3. You will see the rider in a correct jumping seat.

You will need first to shorten your stirrup leathers so that your knee comes up into the knee roll. The knee roll should help the rider's leg stay in position. Suitable saddles are discussed in Chapter 1. Now take your shoulders forward and down towards the horse's shoulders, making sure you bend from the hip and not the waist. Keep your spine in its normal curve as any rounding of your back will weaken your position and cause you to become loose in the saddle. Your seat when in a forward position is *slightly* out of the saddle.

You will find your reins are now too long, so shorten them, still maintaining a straight line elbow, hand, horse's mouth. Strive also to maintain the "elastic" rein contact as you would in your normal position, even though your hands are further along the horse's neck. As I have said, this forward position may feel odd at first but with persistence you will soon become used to it.

Figure 12-1 The Author Riding a Novice Horse

DIAGRAM 16 Correct — Rider in Balance with Horse

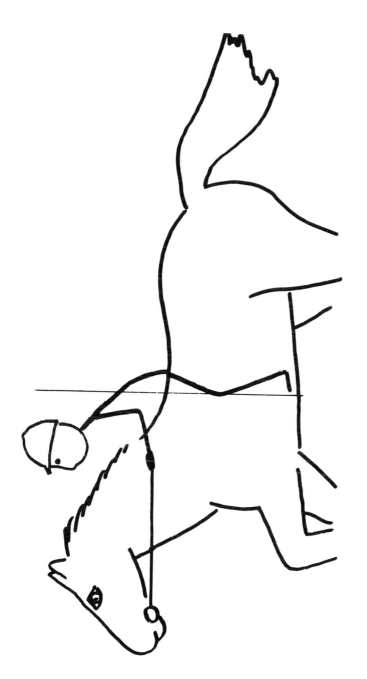

DIAGRAM 17 Incorrect

Note: Rider bending forward from waist instead of hip. Hands too low therefore loss of contact on horse's mouth. Lower leg too far back prevents rider giving correct leg aids. The legs push back and up instead of inwards and forwards. Horse will go along but not truly forward.

PROBLEMS WITH THIS POSITION

Head and Shoulders

In being forward, take care not to round the shoulders and look down; this will cause you to overbalance and drop your hands below the horse's line of contact.

Hands

You may at first experience difficulty in keeping your hands level and steady, particularly if your horse is inclined to be excitable. As a temporary measure try either: (a) resting both hands (on the knuckles) on the horse's neck; or (b) keep the inside hand (knuckles) on the horse's neck and raise the outside one about six inches higher. The raised hand assists in controlling the pace whilst the inside hand remains steady. This is particularly useful in the canter as it prevents the rider pulling back with the inside rein against the leading leg.

Back

When you begin riding in a forward position, you will find your back will ache. Be sure to keep your spine in its normal curve. If you find this difficult, push your seat further back and think of hollowing your back.

Stiffness in the Back may cause the rider either to become "left behind" or collapse his upper body forward on the landing side of the fence.

Legs

The thigh and knee should fit snug onto the saddle. If you find your knee keeps turning away from the saddle, correct this by taking hold of the back of the thigh with your hand, turning the hip joint and rolling the knee in. Push your heel well down and turn the toe slightly out. This will give extra security and strength to your lower leg.

If you are stiff in the ankle and therefore have difficulty in keeping the heel down, do the relevant exercises as suggested in Chapter 2. The rider who cannot keep his heel down and lower leg still, will find his lower leg will continually slide back. This will make his forward driving aids ineffective and cause his upper body to tip too far forward.

GYMNASTIC JUMPING

A chart is given overleaf to assist you in setting out the progressive jumping exercises. The distances given are only intended as a guide.

They may vary according to your horse's shape, his length of stride and state of training of both horse and rider. They will also be affected by the speed and according to whether you approach in walk, trot or canter. The distances between fences must be altered with care. It is a good idea to keep a written account of your horse's progress throughout the exercises. You should find as time goes on that you will be able to make more alterations in your horse's pace and length of stride without upsetting him. From this you will gradually form your own ideas and develop your own system of training. *Always* remember that most problems which occur when jumping can be related to the horse's way of going on the flat. It is a good idea, when attempting anything new, to have a more experienced person to help you. Even the top riders will have someone "on the ground" who can observe them and give advice when needed. If you have any problems with a particular obstacle or series of obstacles, go back first to flat work, then begin again with a simpler exercise and work up again. (See Diagrams which follow, 18—27).

MORE ABOUT JUMPING

If you have been following and putting into practise the previous chapters on flat work and athletic exercises, then the move on to jumping actual courses should not present too much of a problem. However, human nature being what it is, there are bound to be setbacks *en route.* In this chapter I will give some advice about tackling courses and how to prepare for this at home.

SHOW JUMPS

You may be fortunate enough to be able to use ready-made facilities, either in an indoor school, outdoor arena or suitable well drained field. If not and the space you have for schooling is limited and not ideal, then you will need to plan just how and where you are able to practise over fences.

If your intention is to compete in show jumping competitions, then unless you are already a very skilful rider you will need to find somewhere to practise over a course of at least seven obstacles. There are jumps available for hire in most areas, though you may consider this too expensive (especially with the ever-increasing cost of transportation) to do on a regular basis. Although I am neither a carpenter nor an official course builder and have not attempted to go into detail on these subjects, I would like to offer advice, as it affects the average horse owner.

PROGRESSIVE EXERCISES USING POLES AND SMALL OBSTACLES OR CAVELETTI

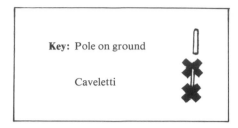

Key: Pole on ground

Caveletti

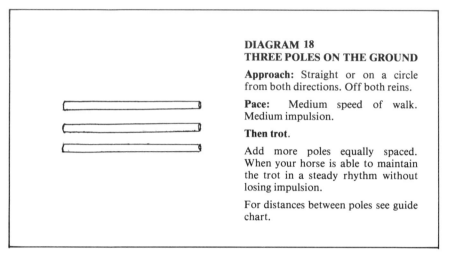

DIAGRAM 18
THREE POLES ON THE GROUND

Approach: Straight or on a circle from both directions. Off both reins.

Pace: Medium speed of walk. Medium impulsion.

Then trot.

Add more poles equally spaced. When your horse is able to maintain the trot in a steady rhythm without losing impulsion.

For distances between poles see guide chart.

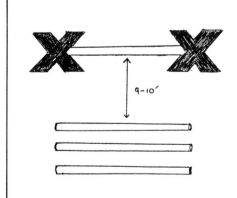

DIAGRAM 19
THREE POLES ON THE GROUND
Followed by a Slightly Raised Pole or Caveletti

Approach: Straight or on a circle. From both reins and either direction.

Pace: Trot, medium speed. Maintain speed and impulsion.

N.B. If your horse becomes excited during this exercise then do it at walk. Maintain a firm but steady rein contact.

For distances see guide chart.

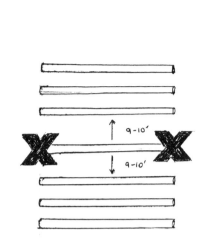

DIAGRAM 20
AS 18 THEN ADD THREE POLES ON THE GROUND

Especially good for horses who are inclined to rush their fences. The poles *after* the obstacle will encourage the horse to steady his pace.

Approach: Either direction, both reins.

Pace: Trot or walk. Plenty of impulsion.

N.B. When laying poles on the ground after a fence make sure the horse is first able to land and see the poles.

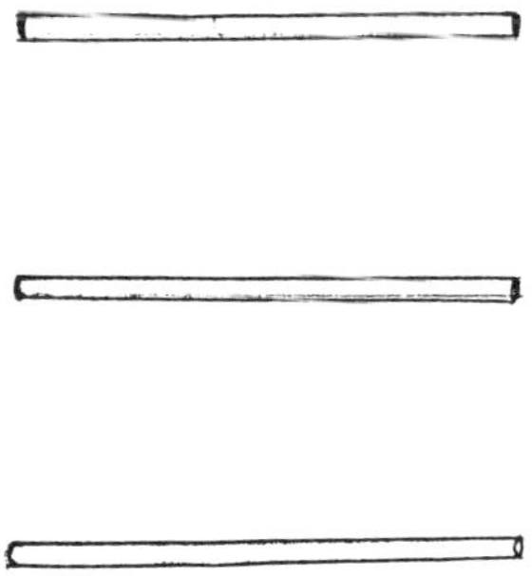

DIAGRAM 21
POLES ON THE GROUND

Approach: Straight or on a circle. Both reins and either direction.

Pace: Canter, medium speed and plenty of impulsion.

N.B. Do not pull or jerk your horse back on the approach as this will tend to confuse or excite him. Allow the horse to work out the striding for himself. Do not drop the contact but try and maintain a consistent 'elastic' hold.

For persistent problems improve the quality of the canter. (See Chapter) Try also repeating the previous exercises.

Distances: Begin with equidistant spacing between poles. See guide chart.

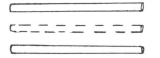

**DIAGRAM 22
TWO OR THREE POLES ON
THE GROUND, A SINGLE
CAVELETTI AND TWO
CAVELETTI TOGETHER TO
FORM A SMALL SPREAD:**

Approach: Straight or on a large circle. From both reins, either direction.

Pace: Trot or if centre pole (marked with a broken line) is removed canter. More impulsion than previous exercises as horse has further to travel.

Distances: Trot poles plus non-jumping, one stride or two stride. Vary these with care.

**DIAGRAM 23
JUMP, POLE, JUMP,
POLE, JUMP:**

Approach: As 5.

Pace: Also as 5.

Distances: Non-jumping, one or two strides. Again vary with care. Make sure and successfully complete each alteration before attempting another.

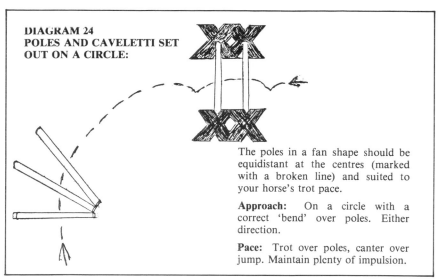

DIAGRAM 24
POLES AND CAVELETTI SET OUT ON A CIRCLE:

The poles in a fan shape should be equidistant at the centres (marked with a broken line) and suited to your horse's trot pace.

Approach: On a circle with a correct 'bend' over poles. Either direction.

Pace: Trot over poles, canter over jump. Maintain plenty of impulsion.

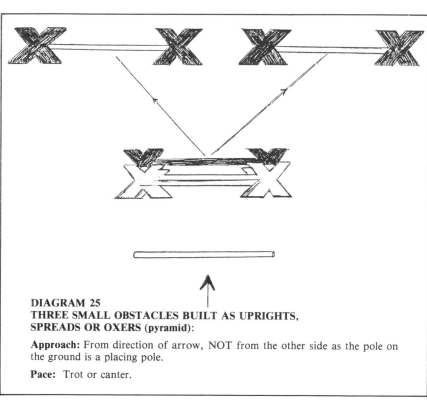

DIAGRAM 25
THREE SMALL OBSTACLES BUILT AS UPRIGHTS, SPREADS OR OXERS (pyramid):

Approach: From direction of arrow, NOT from the other side as the pole on the ground is a placing pole.

Pace: Trot or canter.

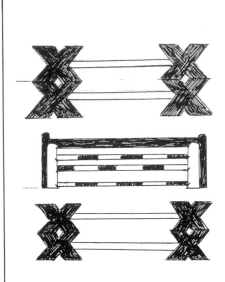

**DIAGRAM 26
CAVELETTI OR
SMALL OBSTACLE**

Set out upright, spread, upright.
OR spread, upright, spread.

Pace: Canter.

Distance: One or two strides, or vary.

N.B. Plenty of impulsion is required for this exercise. If you have been taking your horse successfully through these exercises you will have developed a feel for the natural rhythm of his paces. You should now also know how to set out the exercises to suit your horse's length of stride.

The horse should be increasing in confidence and fluency. He will have begun to use his whole body with greater ease, actually looking at his fences, assessing his own length of stride and making his own adjustments of balance.

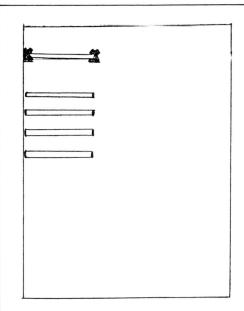

DIAGRAM 27
USEFUL EXERCISES

If you have a small paddock or jumping area you might like to set out some of the exercises alongside the hedge or fence. These could be used for lungeing or loose schooling or for practising your own jumping position.

N.B. If you do attempt any of these do have experienced help. Take care when setting out jumps close to a fence that —

a) The fence itself is not made of barbed wire or the like which could damage horse or rider in in the event of either falling against it.

b) You do not build jumps close to the fence yet leave a small space where the horse could squeeze through and knock himself or his rider.

Note:

The athletic or gymnastic exercises set out in this section are intended for the average horse owner who probably has little space and a limited amount of equipment available. Make sure you move your jumps frequently if you value your ground.

CHART FOR ATHLETIC EXERCISES

	Up to 12.2	Up to 13.2	Up to 14.2	Up to 15.2	Over 15.2	Nature of Obstacle
Walk & Trot	2 ft. 9 in.—3 ft. 0 in.	3 ft. 3 in.	3 ft. 6 in.	4 ft. 0 in.	4 ft. 3 in.	Poles on Ground
Canter Bounce Pace	3 ft. 0 in.—3 ft. 6 in.	4 ft.—4 ft.	6 ft.—7 ft.	9 ft—10 ft.	10 ft.—12 ft.	Raised obstacles All same height
Canter One Stride	18 ft.	18 ft.	18 ft.—21 ft.	21 ft.—24 ft.	24 ft.—26 ft.	As above
Canter Two Strides	21 ft.	24 ft.	28 ft.—30 ft.	31 ft.—34 ft.	33 ft.—36 ft.	As above

The schooling area you use should be at least the size of a dressage arena (see Chapter 6) so why not make three or four jumps of your own?

You will need:

Sufficient poles, wings and fillers to be able to set up the sort of fences you are likely to encounter in competition.

Wings:

There are many types for sale to suit all pockets. Bales, barrels and wood or polystyrene blocks may be used as wings or fillers. Make sure you do not leave bales in the paddock where you turn out horses. If barrels are used to rest poles on, make sure they are prevented from rolling by placing pieces of wood or similar to hold them steady.

Other Fillers:

Plastic fertilizer sacks stuffed with straw, sheep hurdles, pieces of solid boarding painted to simulate a brick wall or other colourful and substantial looking objects.

Poles:

Can be purchased ready made and painted, or you may wish to buy direct from the Forestry Commission. In this case, choose poles which have lain for a year or so as they will not be so heavy. If you paint your own poles, make sure you use a non-toxic paint.

Other Useful "Padding" for fences are old car tyres, small empty containers (providing they did not hold anything toxic), and brush or broom from the hedgerows.

These should be sufficient for a start. Later, as you become more professional, you may wish to add some more fences. If you do wish to add to your course, you can make your own or seek professional advice on course building. There are books available which give sound information on this subject.

SETTING OUT AND RIDING YOUR SHOW JUMPS

You may wish to compete or just become capable enough to give your horse an all-round education. Whichever is the case, let us look at some ways of setting out our limited number of obstacles in a small area.

SHORT COURSES

If you wish to jump your fences from both directions, make sure you do not leave poles on the landing side of the fence, or that there are no poles under the top pole on the descending side in which the horse could become entangled.

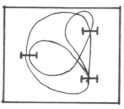
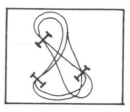
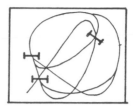

As these are a follow on from the gymnastic exercises, you should by now have become familiar with your horse's length of stride. You will also have some idea as to his capability regarding height and width of fences and angle of turns.

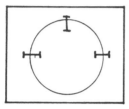
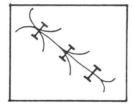
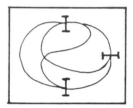

The jumps should be fairly low as the emphasis should be on the way they are ridden and NOT on seeing how high the horse can jump!

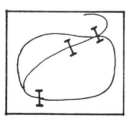
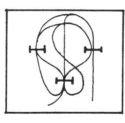
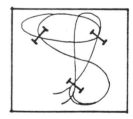

Distances between Doubles. Horse or pony should only take one stride.

13.2 and under 18 ft.
15.HH and under 21 ft.
Over 15 HH 24 ft - 26 ft.

Widen or lengthen distances between fences to suit your horse but do bear in mind if you wish to compete you must be able to meet the specified distances.

DIAGRAM 28 Short Courses

Figure 12-2 Using Caveletti

SAFETY IN YOUR JUMPING AREA

As already stressed in Chapter 3, safety MUST be a prime concern. Make sure there are no protrusions either on the jumps, wings or on your boundary fence which could cause injury. Also, do not leave wing cups or brackets lying anywhere on the ground where they could be trodden or fallen on. Do not build unsafe obstacles; these include fillers which are very flimsy or have gaps in which the horse could get a foot stuck, and wings which are of flimsy construction, or are likely to fall over easily. Do not leave the ends of nails sticking out or use broken wings (a sharp piece of wood could cause severe injury to you or your horse.)

THE RIDER'S JUMPING POSITION ON THE MOVE AND WHILST JUMPING

The novice rider should strive to remain in the forward position as much as possible until he becomes stronger through the thigh and back muscles and more mobile through the pelvis and hip.

You will soon find yourself able to adapt your upper body position according to the type of horse, its state of training, and the sort of fences you are jumping. For instance, on a horse that is inclined to be a bit slow or lacking in confidence, an upright body position will enable you to "get behind" him and drive him forward. A horse which tends to become over excited or is rather strong in the hand is often best ridden in a forward seat.

THE POSITION OVER OBSTACLES:

When negotiating jumps on level ground, make sure you keep shoulders and hips level and do not lean over on turns, particularly at speed. As the horse approaches and takes off over the jumps, try to concentrate on the following:

1. Think more about the horse than yourself. IF you think solely of yourself and leaning forward, you will be more likely to cause the horse to stop. Better to concentrate on maintaining rein contact, legs on and NOT leaning forward too much.
2. Try to remember the way the horse jumps the fence, i.e. smoothly, out of his stride, and working into the rounded topline that you have been creating on the flat, is largely the result of your progressive schooling.

JUMPS UP AND DOWN HILL

The rider's prime concern is to maintain as much impulsion as possible without making the horse become upset. Your aim also is to remain in balance with him. This involves leaning more forward to go uphill and upright when riding downhill. When jumping drop fences (those where the landing side is lower than the take off) you will probably have to take the upper body back and loosen the reins from the highest point of the jump to the ground. Throughout all changes in the upper body position, try to keep the lower leg and thigh firmly in place so that you maintain your balance and ability to apply effective leg aids.

SCHOOLING OVER FENCES AT HOME AND COPING WITH PROBLEMS

Very low obstacles — that is, two feet three inches or under, may be ridden at a walk or trot. Jumping from a walk requires greater impulsion (but little speed) and should not be attempted by complete novices.

By beginning with low obstacles, should your horse refuse at a jump for whatever reason, you have no need to turn away from it. Any horse should be able to scramble over a small jump from practically a standstill. Make sure you never pull the horse backwards in order to give the horse space — remember firstly that a step backwards in competition constitutes a refusal. And secondly, if you insist that he negotiates the obstacle, you instill the idea that if you have asked him to go in a certain direction (whatever the situation) then he must trust you enough to do so. The same applies to ditches, small banks, etc.

JUMPING FROM TROT

This requires a steady rhythm, as much impulsion as you can cope with, and straightness.

Aim to Jump the Centre of the Fence

If your horse tends to be one-sided (see Chapter 8) you will find he will lean towards his "stiff" side on the approach and over the fences. Horses which swerve or run out generally do so towards the "stiff" side. The answer to this is to improve his suppleness, particularly on the "stiff" side, by the schooling exercises given in the previous chapters.

A temporary correction, if you feel the horse fall or lean to one side on the approach to the jump, is to increase contact on both reins, but the rein on the stiff side will feel "heavier" as the horse is leaning more of his weight towards it. You may find it a help also to raise the hand on the stiff side. With the increase in rein contact must come a more active leg aid. Carry your whip also on the stiff side, to reinforce your leg aids, if necessary.

You may feel concerned that a tighter rein contact will cause the horse to refuse or run out. This is unlikely to happen unless you use the rein in a rough or restrictive manner. More refusals and runouts are caused by riders *giving* with the hand just IN FRONT of the jump instead of on the take off. This means that at the very moment when the horse needs the most support from his rider he is dropped, and subsequently tips forward onto his forehand making take off very difficult, even impossible. Correct contact is particularly important when approaching a fence downhill or on a curve. Jumps into water and combinations of fences also need steady and balanced riding.

N.B. Obviously as your flatwork improves and your horse develops both physically and mentally, the effect on your jumping will become most apparent.

JUMPING FROM CANTER

The quality of the canter is vital, particularly for show jumping, where the horse needs to be able to adjust his length of stride and his balance in a relatively small area. The canter work given in Chapter 9 will help towards this aim and will also give you a feel of your horse's length of stride. This in turn will help you to see a stride into a fence, and so judge just where your horse will take off. Eventually you will find yourself able to make adjustments on the approach to a fence, so making jumping less of a hit and miss affair!

SEEING A STRIDE

To be able to judge the number of strides the horse will make before taking off over a jump can take the rider some considerable time. If you experience this difficulty, try the following:—

1. Lay out three poles well spaced around the perimeter of your schooling area and set off in canter over them. At each canter stride say out loud "NOW, NOW, NOW", *or* sing a song which fits in with your horse's rhythm. Try "Half a pound of tuppenny rice", etc. You will find yourself beginning to adjust your horse's stride to fit into the rhythm of the song and his "jumps" over the poles. Singing or talking when you ride also helps you to breathe more evenly when you feel tense). As you become proficient using the poles, replace them first with cavellitti and then with jumps.

   N.B. Remember the length of time spent in canter must be according to the fitness of horse and rider.

2. You could also have your instructor, or an experienced friend, watch you and count the last three, four or five strides into the jump for you.

3. You may also find that if you sit upright on the last few strides into the jump you will be able to see the stride more easily.

4. A groundline (a pole on the ground just in front of the jump) may also help.

5. Also, a placing pole (a pole on the ground one canter stride in front of the jump).

ACROSS COUNTRY

The canter needs to be faster and bigger striding. More impulsion is therefore required. The ability of the rider and horse to adjust without losing the forward impetus is very important across country. To ride on as fast as possible is not only foolhardy, but extremely dangerous.

Fences out in the open which can be clearly seen by the horse will only need the minimum of half-halts on approach. The more obscure obstacles need less speed, more leg and a stronger "elastic" rein contact. They require the rider to be very much "with" his horse and ready to alter the amount of leg or rein at a split second's notice.

Difficult Obstacles

Among the more difficult obstacles (regardless of height), are:

1. **Jumping into a Wood**

   Jumping from light into dark can be a problem if the horse has never done this before. It helps considerably if he has confidence in his rider.

2. **Jumping Up and Down Banks,** through combinations of ditches and rails, "alternative" fences where the route through must be carefully planned by the rider.

3. **Jumps into Water,** which even if fairly shallow, will slow the horse down very quickly indeed. If you do ride too fast into water you are very likely to tip the horse and yourself over!

4. **Negotiating Jumps through a Narrow Path** in a wood or similar. It is important to maintain impulsion and an even rhythm, either in canter or a strong trot, according to the experience of yourself or your horse.

5. **Angled Approaches** can be tricky. If you lose straightness or impulsion, or lose your horse's concentration, or make the

Figure 12-3 Showing Harmony Between Horse and Rider

angle too acute, then you will cause the horse to run out.

See overleaf ideas for setting out a maximum variety of cross country obstacles on a small area.

SUMMARY

THE RIDER'S AIMS

The basic schooling is hard work, both for horse and rider. The rider needs an enormous amount of tact, sensitivity and unwavering determination to succeed. (The preceding chapters of this book should help you to assess if you are on the right track).

The aims are:
1. The rider is striving to establish and maintain a basically correct but natural position on his horse, as described in the early chapters of this book.
2. He should be able to apply controlled effective aids, and begin to form some "mental" rapport with his horse.
3. He should have begun to develop a "feel" of the effect his body weight and aids have upon his horse. This will enable him to improve his horse, both on the flat and over fences.

The rider should be able to extract the following from his horse:
   (a) Forward impulsive, rhythmical work at walk, trot and canter.
   (b) The horse should work with even strides on both reins and be equally supple in both directions.
   (c) The transitions should be smooth and forward going. The horse should maintain a steady neck and head position. Towards the completion of the horse's basic training, the transitions should become more immediate.

COMPETITIONS

Horse and rider should now be ready, should you desire, to compete in any of the following:
1. *Prix Caprilli* — is a straightforward riding test judged on the rider's position, his correct application of the aids and "feel" on his horse.
2. **Preliminary and novice dressage competitions** are becoming increasingly popular with riders. The tests cover the movements as described in this book and are judged mainly on the way the horse goes, with a mark and comment at the end for the rider.

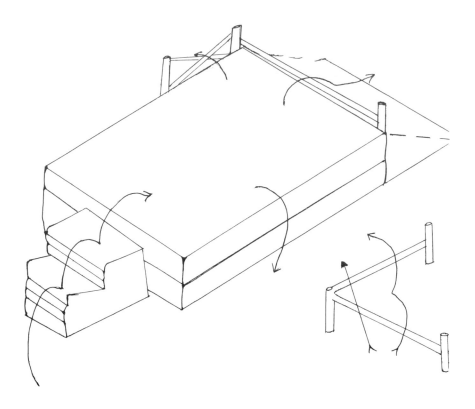

DIAGRAM 29 Construction of Bank

Note:

A bank can be constructed from a heap of earth (make sure it does not contain any injurous material). Then either, leave it for a period to settle; e.g. 1 year) or pack it down. The sides can be sloping or supported by railway sleepers. Keep the bank long and low and you can incorporate a variety of obstacles on and near it. A bank of this sort could be especially useful to jumping enthusiasts with a small amount of space at their disposal.

3. **Riding Horse, Family Pony Classes, Utility Horse** — judged on suitability of horse or pony as an all-round sensible animal.
4. **Showing** — there are classes for all breeds and types of horse and pony. These tend to be very competitive, especially at the bigger shows.
5. **Jumping**
   Those new to competing should begin with unaffiliated classes, such as clear round or novice. This applies to cross country as well as show jumping.
6. **Gymkhana**
   Mounted games, mainly for those under 18 years of age, are great fun. They give children experience, co-ordination and confidence.
7. **Eventing**
   Combines dressage, show-jumping and cross-country riding. For skilled riders, requires also a thorough knowledge of fitness and feeding.
8. **Dressage with Jumping**
   Competitors ride a dressage test and jump a round of show jumps. Penalties incurred whilst jumping are deducted from the dressage score to find the prize winners.
9. **Long-Distance Riding** — is now a sport in its own right and also entails a deep knowledge of fitness of horse and rider.

There are also other activities open to riders. These are polo, hunting, riding holidays where you may take your own horse, instructional courses; etc.

FINAL ADVICE TO RIDERS

Go and watch any acitivities or competitions before you attempt any. Make sure you know all the rules and regulations. These can be obtained by writing to the British Horse Society.

Good luck and many hours of happy riding!

INDEX

INDEX